Raising Smart & Kind Kids

Early Education and Teaching Empathy

Part of the

77 Ways to Parent Series

By Judy H. Wright

Aka Auntie Artichoke

Raising Smart & Kind Kids

Self-published in the United States of America by:

ARTICHOKE PRESS LLC

Medical Disclaimer: Please use this book as a guide and suggestions, not as medical or psychological advice. Judy H. Wright is not a doctor, licensed counselor or professional consultant. She is a parent educator and family advocate. If you are concerned about some aspect of your child's development, or your own mental health, do not hesitate to seek professional help.

Affiliate Disclaimer: Some of the resources and programs that are recommended in this eBook pay a small commission to the author when you buy them. This commission is used to further the goals of those who protect children, so we appreciate your support. You pay the same amount, but the company pays Artichoke Press for the referral.

Acknowledgements

My deepest admiration, love and amazement go to those Moms, Dads, Grams, Aunties and Uncles who have helped me recognize how special each child is. Of course, their particular loved one is wonderfully talented. I am grateful they have allowed me to hear the stories, see the pictures and share in the community and village that helps raise these smart and kind kids.

A special thank you goes to three very special moms:

- **Bethany Wright Loosli** who is running a living laboratory of loving care for our precious grandkids. She and the little kids are forever teaching me new ways of looking at things.
- **Theresa LeCoultre** who has been my technical brains and formatting genius for over a year. A single mom who runs a business and a family well.
- **Molly Stockdale** who has just recently been guided to assist in the editing and expansion of the ideas of early childhood. PTO president, room mother & mom.

These good women have been through almost everything you are going through with your children and lived to laugh about it. So take hope and realize you don't have to be a perfect parent (as if there really were such creatures) but you do want to be a present parent. Just showing up every day is 90% of the game plan.

Dedicated with love

to my children and grandchildren

who have taught me so much in life.

Raising Smart & Kind Kids

I am a great believer in the Law of Attraction; you were drawn to this book for a reason.

May you find the answers that will touch your heart and enhance your family relationships.

Please take note that I am not a doctor, psychologist, neuroscientist, perfect parent, or researcher on how brains work. I am a mom, gram-cracker, auntie, and parent educator. Our home has been a safe haven for many kids who did not have good parenting.

Hopefully you are looking for an affordable, common sense booklet to help teach or remind you of how to connect with your baby. Welcome and keep reading.

My name is Judy H. Wright and I live with my husband Dwain in beautiful Missoula, Montana where we have raised our children and been active in the community for many years.

We have six wonderful adult children and ten really wonderful grandchildren scattered all over the country. I have written many, many books and articles, and have spoken all over the world about finding the heart of the story in the journey of life.

However, my proudest accomplishment is that my family members like themselves and each other.

Please think of me as an approachable neighbor or wise, kind and caring auntie that you have turned to for advice.

Be comfortable and open to these suggestions and know that I want only the best for you and yours. You are a good and loving parent who wants to find solutions to daily irritants and problems or you wouldn't have purchased this series of **77 Ways to Parent**.

I have been a parent educator and family coach for many years. I work with Head Start families and childcare providers, as well as parents and teachers just like you. **Yes, you are a teacher.** Every one of us is teaching the next generation, whether we want to or not.

We can either teach them by using "encouraging words" or "discouraging words." Using encouragement is the gift of courage to keep trying. It is about the process of growing and developing rather than being focused on the end result. I have included a list of encouraging words at the back of the book. Many parents tell me that hey have never heard encouragement directed to them and so they don't know the words to say. ***Now you will!***

Those of us who care deeply about the children in our circle of influence need to teach them the values, ethics and standards that will help them to live successful and happy lives.

We are parents and caring adults, you and I. We are equals and will treat each other and the children with respect and kindness. I am part of the village that cares about you and your children.

The great majority of parents really do care about our kids and want the best for them. Sure we do thoughtless and unkind things occasionally.

Of course we get cranky and stressed and impatient and fall back into old patterns of behavior until someone reminds us to do better and try harder.

This book is not aimed toward the doctor, neuroscientist etc. but toward parents who need an affordable reminder to engage with their kids. If you came from a loving home, you may know everything contained here. Most of it is common sense, but in life common sense is not so common. Many parents were not parented well as children and need suggestions, tips and methods of bonding with their child. The rest of us just need to be reminded of fun ways to connect.

We always say our kids survived and prospered in spite of everything we did wrong. It is never too late to sincerely apologize for forgetting the class play and for embarrassing the Brownie troop by wearing the wrong clothes. They will eventually forgive you for yelling at them when you were really just mad at the situation.

Grab a cup of tea, and enjoy the next few minutes sharing ideas and tips to make life easier.

You deserve the best and I am confident in your ability to impact the world by influencing your children to make wise choices.

Your child is a spiritual being in a human body. Do what you can to encourage his spirit and you will be successful as a parent and student. This little child has come to you to teach and guide you more than you need to teach him or her.

Think good thoughts, smile a lot and enjoy your life. It is meant to be lived in joy.

Love,

Judy Helm Wright

RAISING SMART & KIND KIDS: *THE BABY YEARS*...... 4

Raising Smart & Kind Kids: *The Baby Years*

From the moment a sperm and egg connect, that developing person has a unique personality, learning style as well as likes and dislikes. No matter how many children you have, you find that each one is a different individual and what works with one, will not even be noticed by another.

When your baby is in the womb, it has an ideal environment in which to expand and grow. The space is perfect for their full potential. It has nourishment, safety, and boundaries and meets all their needs. It has everything they need to not only survive, but to thrive.

And then they outgrow it and are evicted

But, the new home is so loving and kind and the landlords think the new member is wonderful, beautiful, smart, perfect, and made just for their home and family. Hopefully, the village is excited to love and nurture this new member into their society and tribe.

Developing Brains

At birth, the infant's brain has 100 billion nerve cells, or neurons. These neurons will grow and connect to form systems that enhance various functions like seeing, hearing, moving and expressing emotion.

The parts of the brain that handle thinking and remembering, as well as emotional and social behavior are very underdeveloped at birth. The brain is present at birth, but matures in the world rather than the womb.

Our job as caring adults is to care for everything that baby needs in the environment of our home and child care situations. We have an individual growing and developing towards full potential. We now have to physically, emotionally, and spiritually provide for their experiences. We are responsible for their nourishment, safety, boundaries and loving environment.

The brain is the part of the body that allows us to feel joy or despair, to respond to others in loving or angry ways. This wonderful organ helps us not only understand what an apple is and how it tastes, but to think of ways to get the apple to our mouth.

A baby's relationship with parents and other important caregivers is very critical for a happy, fulfilling life. The sights, sounds, smells, touches, experiences and activities don't just affect their moods. These experiences' actually affect the way the brain becomes "wired."

The guidelines and techniques we are going to discuss in this book are generalities and overviews. You are the one who will personalize it for your baby. You are the expert on your baby. No one knows and loves your child as you do. Trust your instincts and enjoy this special journey of life with your new companion.

Even though your baby or toddler may not have language to express wants and desires, there are clues if you watch for them. I challenge you to tune in to their expressions, movements and babbling. Observe, listen and understand what and how your child learns by paying attention and looking at things from their point of view.

Teach and be Taught

A baby is the most responsive and rewarding pupil you will ever have. He wants to do more, explore, touch, feel, smell, taste, hear, and see everything in his environment.

Initially, the most important people in a baby's life are the one or two who most consistently look after him. In most cases, these are the parents. In other words, you are the most important teacher your child will ever have, just as he is your most important pupil.

As adults, we learn the most from people we like, trust, respect and have developed a special rapport with. When we recognize that the feelings are mutual, magic happens. When all the components click, we are like sponges and the message is like a lesson. These lessons remain with us for a lifetime.

Those of us who have loving people in our lives to help us learn critical thinking skills are very fortunate. We feel valued, empowered, and much more open to stretching to the limits. It is as if we have been handed a *huge gift of courage*.

That is my definition of encouragement. We are not afraid to take risks, because we know we are loved unconditionally and accepted for who and what we are.

Our relationship with caring adults is not based on how well we perform, obey or make someone else happy. It is a mutually empowering and respectful union.

Benefits of Breastfeeding

How long do you breast feed your baby? Will it make your breasts hang low? Will it limit sex if your breasts leak during foreplay? Will it mean that mom and dad can never go out on a date without bringing baby along? Will my husband still think I am sexy when he sees me breastfeeding? What happens when I go back to work?

All of these valid questions have come from parenting classes that I have held with parents just like you. Both moms and dads have concerns and questions about why to breastfeed their infant. I recognize that quandary; you want what is best for your baby, but you would still like to have a personal life.

The American Academy of Pediatrics recommends breastfeeding for at least twelve months. Too many families fall short of that goal and by five or six months only 30 percent of babies are still being breastfed.

The greatest reason more families don't continue breastfeeding for at least a year is lack of support. Many moms give up because they don't know anyone who has breastfed a baby, or they don't have friends, family, doctors or partners who encourage them to continue.

Breastfeeding your baby has many benefits; for infant, mom, family, economy, community & environment. If you cannot breastfeed or make a choice not to do so, do not feel guilty or less than a loving mom or woman. Whether you choose to feed your baby with breast or bottle, just remember to hold them in a close and loving way. Do not feel guilty if you cannot, or choose not to breastfeed.

Benefits for Breastfeeding Baby

1. Enhances the immune system
2. Reduces the risk of gastroenteritis, lower respiratory tract infections and asthma
3. Protects against allergies and food intolerances
4. Decreases colic and calms the baby more quickly
5. Promotes correct jaw and tooth alignment
6. Babies who breastfeed test out with a higher IQ and enhanced school performance through adolescence
7. There is a marked decrease in the development of several auto-immune diseases
8. Reduces the risk of obesity, heart disease, hypertension, high cholesterol and childhood leukemia
9. Reduces the risk of SIDS (sudden infant death syndrome)
10. Increases infant and mother bonding
11. Breast milk protects babies from some of the effects of pollution

Benefits For Mom & Family

12. Decreases the risk for chronic diseases such as type 2 diabetes, breast cancer and ovarian cancer
13. Increases your calorie expenditure, which may lead to a quicker return to pre-baby weight
14. Faster shrinking of the uterus
15. Reduces postpartum bleeding and delay the return of the menstrual cycle
16. Decreases the risk of postpartum depression
17. Enhances self-esteem in the maternal role
18. Decreases time and money
19. Lower health care costs ($150 billion increase in medical costs each year in US for formula fed infants)
20. Increases handiness and efficiency
21. Infant formula costs $7 each day or $2,555 for a year. This money can be spent on furniture, clothing, vacations, school or other wants of the family.
22. Breastfed babies waste products and dirty diapers don't smell bad. It is not until food is introduced that the aroma becomes strong.
23. Increases infant and mother bonding and attachment. This attachment will enhance or hinder relationships for the rest of the child's life.
24. It is a wonderful excuse to sit down, put your feet up and just enjoy your baby.

Create a Village or Community

As I teach parenting classes around the country, I ask participants to share "angels, mentors and teachers" who have impacted their lives. All the people who touch our lives or the lives of our children have an impact, some more important and long lasting than others. Parents always top the list of important "members of the village", but it is amazing how much impact those who are in our lives only a short time can have.

When a teacher, coach, crossing guard, day care provider, neighbor or librarian shows an interest in the education and life of a child, an even bigger magic happens. It is this sometime pivotal person or experience that shapes a person's destiny.

For Oprah Winfrey, it was the white woman who patted her cheek and said, "You are as cute as a little speckled pup." Oprah says it was the first time she had ever known she was attractive. She had been complimented on being smart, but it was one kind pat and a few kind words that changed her outlook on her life.

So as your child grows and develops, plan on incorporating a "village or community of caring" to help them reach full potential. Others will enhance and add to the work you have done in building a foundation of awareness and a love of learning.

Why Everyone Loves Babies

We all love to associate with and watch babies because they encounter life through their senses. As caring adults we get to vicariously experience the world anew through taste, sight, touch, sound, smell and instinct. Each positive interaction gives them opportunities to stimulate their senses. We are already becoming involved in making them smart, simply by doing simple everyday things and then watching with wonder as they blossom and grow.

Early care has a lifelong impact on how our babies develop their ability to learn. Early enrichment and loving care lead to healthy brain development. On the other hand exposure to domestic violence, neglect and abuse may cause some genetically normal children to have developmental delays.

Nourishing and Nurturing Environment

In my training, it has been emphasized that there can be harmful and long-lasting effects on unborn babies and young children when they are exposed to an environment in which adults are using nicotine, alcohol, and/or mind-altering drugs. Living in chaotic homes, many infants do not receive the support and care, which will help them develop the brain, networks.

Scientists once thought genetics determined brain development but recent studies are indicating that brain growth is particularly dependent on the infant's early experiences with primary caregivers.

John Bradshaw in *The Family-A New Way Of Creating Solid Self Esteem* (Health Communications) describes a healthy family environment as:

""A healthy family environment provides the opportunity for all members to get their needs met insofar as that is possible.

Each person needs:

- Self-worth, self-love, self-acceptance and the freedom to be the unique and unrepeatable one that he is.
- Touching and mirroring.
- Structure that is safe enough to risk growth and individuation; such a structure will change according to the stages of one's development.
- Affection and recognition.

14

- His feelings affirmed.
- Challenge and stimulation to move though each stage of development/
- Self-actualization and spirualization. This means the opportunity to live for something greater than oneself."

If you are in a position to help parents who cannot seem to cope with life or are neglecting their children, please step forward.

It may be as simple as sharing ideas with other parents in the park or modeling loving care towards their child.

Hopefully, it will not be necessary to involve "the system" but your actions could save the life of a child.

My simple technique is to compliment the parents of every child I see; "You have a beautiful child (or children.) In my mind, at least, I think that if parents realize that other adults are noticing and complimenting their family, they will be more kind and loving towards them. May not work all the time, but, don't you like to be complimented on your child?

Read, Sing and Talk To Your Baby

When babies make cooing sounds, we make cooing sounds in return. When they smile, we smile and then they smile and it goes on and on. Our job is to provide prompt responses to his needs, consistent care and love. Hopefully, we will share opportunities for activities, which will help move and develop muscles including the brain.

When it is play time, provide a secure, loving relationship; affection, patience and encouragement of his constant activity. When it is food time, the caring adults are excited with each development step and we mirror their expressions of joy when tasting applesauce.

We want to provide as rich an environment with as many positive social and learning opportunities as possible. We want to stimulate those synapses associated with positive experiences to become a permanent part of the child's brain.

In order to do that all caregivers will want to provide a secure, loving relationship which will include affection, patience and encouragement of his constant activity. Rather than scolding or commanding, try gently teaching by reading, singing and talking to your baby.

The more experiences a child has, the more connections its brain cells will make. The size of the baby's brain will almost triple in the first three years of life.

Children who don't have stimulating and enriching experiences such as cuddling, being talked, sung and read to, have underdeveloped brains. Those children will have the same number of cells, but there will be fewer connections between them.

Shut Off The Electronic Baby-Sitter

A very important thing you can do to stimulate your child's brain development is to **shut off the TV.** No matter how educational a show is, and there are some good ones, a child needs interaction and one-on-one attention from a loving and kind adult.

Have I convinced you how important it is to provide caregiving in a nurturing, supportive and safe way? I hope so. Young children need and deserve safety, love, conversation and a stimulating environment to develop and keep these important synapses in the brain.

Do you need tapes, videos, flashcards, lots of money, scheduled time and an agenda to accomplish this important task? Absolutely not!

You need yourself, a few storybooks, some common everyday items from around your house and lots of love and determination to help your baby develop.

Is it too late to start now? No, the brain is growing and developing through experiences. There are some pretty predictable stages; most babies smile at six weeks, crawl at nine months, and walk at 12 months. However, the brain is quite flexible and if any of these or other stages were missed, most circuits are still able to wire up until about 10 years of age.

Guidelines for Growth

As they grow, children are always learning new things. Below are just some of the "bench marks" you should be aware of as your baby grows and develop.

This guide is not written in stone any more than the age each of us reach puberty!

Each child is unique and special and is on his own personal journey in life. As caring parents, keep your eyes and hearts open and you will know intuitively if your child may need additional help or guidance in an area.

This is not a competition. There is no race. Do not allow grandparents, neighbors or other parents make you or your child feel like there is a winner or loser in who walks, talks and says "Mama" first.

If you have concerns, talk with your child's doctor and get connected with your community's early childhood intervention system.

At 6 months, a child will probably be able to:

- Hold up his head
- Follow moving object with his eyes
- Focus his eyes on small object
- Begin to reach for objects
- Respond to his own name
- Respond to another's emotions and try to copy sounds
- Like to play games
- Transfer objects from one hand to another
- Say one sound repeatedly
- Smile, giggle and laugh
- Show eagerness by making sounds

At 1 year (12 Months), many children will

- Use simple gestures, like shaking head "no" or waving "bye-bye"
- Say "Mama" and "dada" and exclamations like "oh-oh"
- Copy gestures of siblings
- Hold, bite, chew a cracker or a biscuit
- Feed herself with her fingers
- Drink from a cup with help
- Respond to simple spoken requests
- Hold her arms up to be held
- Repeat a performance when laughed at or applauded
- Pick up small toys with thumb and finger.

At 18 months, many children will

- Play simple pretend games, such as feeding a doll
- Point to show others something interesting
- Show a full range of emotions, such as happy, sad, angry
- Say and understand several sing words and sentences
- Follow simple instructions
- Point to things or pictures when they are named

For toddlers and preschoolers, please see my other books in this series available at www.ArtichokePress.com *or at* http://amzn.to/kindlebyjudy

Getting and Staying Connected to Your Baby

Parents all over the world worry about how what they do will affect the way their children turn out as adults. Most successful families have found that healthier attachment infancy is likely to turnout an emotionally healthier adult. How the significant caregivers and the baby connect and interact in the first year together will make a difference for the rest of their life.

To guide and teach your child you have to know and understand the clues and cues of body language, and to respond in a loving and supportive way.

As your initial responses to the infant will be trail and error, they will quickly become intuitive. You will develop of harmony between the cue giving and care-giving.

This is one of the reasons that the primary caregivers be kept to a minimum and those to be consistent in care. It is too disruptive for a baby to try to wonder if this one will understand his cry for a diaper change or needing to burp.

If you are using a day-care system, make sure the caregivers are consistent, kind and nurturing. They should collaborate in a partnership with the parents, grandparents and other loving adults to nurture your child in body, mind and spirit.

Stimulating the Senses

Taste, smell and touch are sometimes called the minor senses. Hearing and seeing are called the major senses. Taste and smell are separate senses and each has different brain regions. However, they influence each other by associations of sensations in the cortex of the brain.

Learning with all five senses + one

During the first three years of life, children experience the world in a more complete way than children of any other age. The brain takes in the external world through its system of sight, hearing, smell, touch and taste.

This means that infant social, emotional, cognitive, and physical and language development are stimulated during multi-sensory experiences. Infants and toddlers need the opportunity to participate in a world filled with stimulating sights, sounds and people.

I like to add the sense of self, because it is vital that each one us be in tune with our own intuition and guidance system. This sense of trusting your instincts and of following the promptings of your  spirit will help your child to make wise decisions and be more aware of danger.

Never forget the importance of the emotional side of everything. Even though I am sharing some great games, they are only vehicles to connect you and your baby. This warm relationship is the most effective way to help a baby learn.

You are the very best toy or learning equipment available in the whole wide world.

Create a multi-sensory environment

- Experiment with different smells in the environment. Try scents like peppermint and cinnamon to keep children alert, and lavender to calm them down.
- Remember that lighting affects alertness and responsiveness. Bright lights keep infants and toddlers alert; soft lights help infants and toddlers to calm down.
- Expose infants and toddlers to colors that stimulate the brain. Use colors like pale yellow, beige and off-white to create a calm learning environment; use bright colors such as red, orange and yellow to encourage creativity and excitement.
- Use quiet and soft music to calm infants and toddlers and rhythmic music to get them excited about moving.
- Create a texture book or board that includes swatches of different fabrics for infants and toddlers to feel.
- Describe the foods and drinks that you serve infants and toddlers and use words that are associated with flavor and texture ("oranges are sweet and juicy;" "lemon yogurt is a little sour and creamy").

25

Thinking and feeling

Before children are able to talk, emotional expressions are the language of relationships. Research shows that infants' positive and negative emotions, and caregivers' sensitive responsiveness to them, can help early brain development.

For example, shared positive emotion between a caregiver and an infant, such as laughter and smiling, engages brain activity in good ways and promotes feelings of security. Also, when interactions are accompanied by lots of emotion, they are more readily remembered and recalled.

Do you remember when a wonderful smell influenced how you thought something would taste?

A long time ago, I was trying to convince my own family to "go vegetarian." I added TSP, a meat substitute made from defatted soy flour, to spaghetti sauce. Our three-year- old came in the door and announced that whatever I was cooking smelled like dog food, and she would rather starve than eat it!

To my knowledge, our daughter had never tasted dog food, and yet the smell triggered such a negative reaction in her brain that I agreed to not expose them to that smell again.

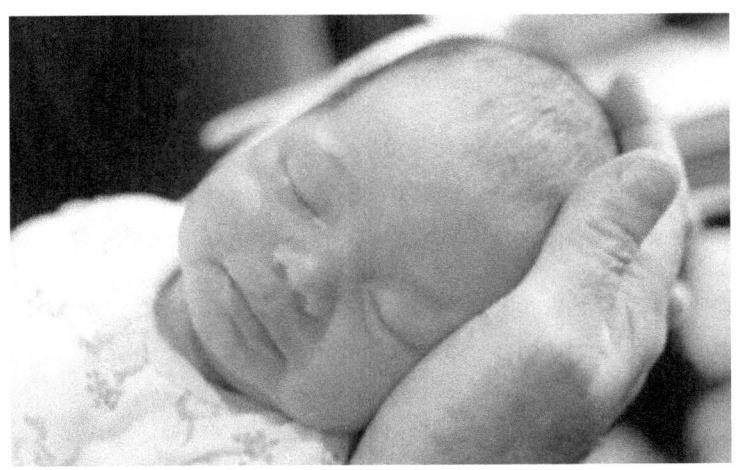

Birth to 3 Months

During this period you will see your baby's first smile and hear the first coos, especially when she sees your face. This is the time that she will start to use sounds and facial expressions to get your attention and respond to your talking.

Babies tend to cry more at 1-3 months than at any other time. Be sure to hold your baby and respond when she cries. Make soothing sounds and gently rub her legs, arms and back. Bring your face into the baby's vision. Swaddle and hold close, rock or walk while singing softly.

Pacifiers may comfort your baby or help them a "lovey" that will help her self-soothe. Caressing the bottom of her feet worked with one of our children when nothing else did.

Babies "communicate" through their behavior, which, although it may not always seem like it, is a rational language. I am always amazed watching new parents who know what calms their baby.

It doesn't take long for you to figure out whether she likes to be held over your shoulder, cuddled in your arm, or draped over your lap.

Dr. Linda Eaglehart is a developmental psychologist and an associate professor of psychology at the University of Montana. She is a fellow member of the Healthy Start Council of the Missoula Forum for Children and Youth, a coalition that helps Missoula, Montana USA kids to be healthy and resilient. Linda recently wrote in our newspaper-

> "A newborn must learn how to get basic needs met. Are her cries for food answered or not? Her parent's response to her needs will teach her important lessons on effective communication with others. If she learns trust, she can explore an environment full of rich stimulation.

> "An infant whose cries go unanswered, hears insensitive words and receives rough treatment may redirect focus on attaining basic needs only. When the focus turns away from exploration, interaction with people and objects may become difficult for the infant. Her brain will ignore important environmental stimulation needed to develop healthy intellectual and social skills when focusing on survival needs."

Clues and Cues From Your Baby

Not only do infants respond to cues around them, for example, a parent's face, but they also take steps to manage their environment, such as crying to get a response from their caregivers. It is cause and effect, not conscious manipulation.

It is a developmental stage to work through as they grow to realize (much later) that they are not the center of the universe. But as infants, they think that when they cry, you will show up. This is as it should be. They need to be hub of the family for a while.

High Risk or High Maintenance Babies

High-risk infants may spend most of their energy trying to maintain a balance in their bodies. Their energy isn't as available to concentrate on growth. In the case of a high-risk infant, it is even more important that you read, sing and talk to this sweet little baby who is working so hard to thrive.

Your baby wants and needs to feel you close by. If he stops crying when you pick him up then he obviously needs cuddling. There are some babies that need to be held all the time (like our second daughter, who actually had an ovarian hernia - but that is another story)

These high maintenance babies seem to do best when the mom or dad "wear" them in a sling or carrier that holds them close to the parent's heart. The baby stays close, feels secure and cries less.

You cannot spoil a newborn baby. In fact, as a parent educator, I have found that if a baby's needs are not met when he is an infant, he might have more serious emotional problems later on in life.

Use your singing voice to tell your child how much you love her. Talk about all the people who form a circle of love around your child. Use your calming and encouraging voice to tell the stories and nursery rhythms you enjoyed as a child.

Again, to quote from Dr. Linda Eaglehart

"Infants who receive sensitive, responsive care from caregiver develop the foundations associated with 'successful' children. The relationships developed with important adults establish the groundwork for healthy emotional development, providing them with some protection from the countless stressors found in childhood.

"Researchers examining life histories of successful children found they had at least one secure, supportive bond with an adult-typically a parent, family member or mentor- in early life."

Modeling Kindness & Empathy

Children will do what you do. Your actions and attitudes are even more important than your words. Children always learn better when there is less anxiety in their environment. It also helps to have a motivation for learning new skills and mastering challenging tasks. With babies, that motivation is as simple as a smile or a kiss from someone who loves you.

Sometimes communication has been divided into two different areas; verbal or spoken words and non-verbal actions or body talk. Verbal language is the means to share information and non-verbal communication is a language of relationships.

We have all encountered someone who says; "No, really. It is just fine." And yet their face and body convey anger, resentment and disappointment. Is there any question which we believed-the words or the actions? Chances are good, we recognized and believed what they did, much more than what they said.

It is important as we communicate with our child we do so with kindness, love and empathy. We want our facial expressions and body language to mirror our loving and encouraging words. Is that possible 100% of the time? Of course not. Parents are human and as humans we get tired, cranky and stressed.

As a mom, gram, auntie and teacher I can empathize with your feelings. My empathy comes from experience but also from learning how to go outside of myself and recognize and acknowledge the feelings that parents go through.

Empathy is the ability to understand another's feelings and emotions.

In researching my books on friendship and also on bullying, (see http://www.ArtichokePress.com) I continually found that children who had learned empathy in the window of up to age seven or eight, were able to see events and circumstances from the other person's viewpoint. If they had not been taught and experienced empathy and kindness before this period, it was almost impossible for them to grasp how their unkindness affected others.

Actually, if they do not understand empathy and kindness by the time they reach adolescence, it will take an active intervention by someone to help them recognize their actions can harm or hurt others.

Name and Claim Emotions

Even though you will find this section in many of my other books, it bears repeating. So many adults do not know how to be authentic about their own feelings. Only when the adults can understand that feelings are not right or wrong, they just are how we are processing our world right now, can we allow our children to recognize the power of true feelings.

Much like the iceberg, the current feeling may be the one that is expressed, while there is a deeper needs down under that is the real problem.

Both words "anger" and "hunger" represent unmet needs. Have you ever had a craving for a comfort food, and then realized it wasn't the food you wanted, but rather the comfort?

So when you are feeling one of the following emotions, stop and ask yourself what is the need that is making you feel that way. Can you put it into words? What are you really hungry for? Is it respect? Is it family members helping around the house? Is it a compliment or acknowledgment of what you have done?

Can you find a solution to that unmet need? Can you figure out what you really need right now? Will you be empowered enough to ask for what you want? Will you be willing to examine what would make you happy? I promise, it is not the cookie or glass of wine.

Words Reflecting "Upset" Feelings

We all need to understand that there are many varying degrees of upset feelings that can be expressed in a way that makes communication easier. It is empowering to be able to name your feelings. When you can accurately describe how you feel, then others can assist you in finding solutions.

Some such examples of feelings you would experience when your needs are not being met:

> *abandoned, accused, angry, annoyed, aggravated, alienated, alone, anxious, bored, confused, defeated, disconnected, difficult, disappointed, discouraged, disgusted, disrespected, doubt, embarrassed, frightened, frustrated, guilty, hate, hopeless, hurt, inadequate, incapable, left out, miserable, put down, panicked, petrified, rejected, sad, stupid, unfair, unhappy, unloved, worried, worthless*

Words Reflecting "Happy" Feelings

Just as there are varying degrees of upset feelings, there are just as many different words to describe happy emotions.

When you use the right words, people know and understand where you are coming from and how to connect with you on a deeper level.

Some examples of positive and upbeat words to describe how you feel when you are in a state of happiness and your needs are being met might be:

> *accepted, affectionate, amused, appreciated, better, capable, comfortable, confident, content, delighted, encouraged, engaged, enjoy, excited, fulfilled, glad, good, grateful, great, happy, hopeful, inspired, joyful, loved, peaceful, pleased, proud, relieved, respected, satisfied, silly*

More ideas to make learning fun

Some of these exercises have been adapted from *125 Brain Games for Babies* by Jackie Silberg. Most have been observed in successful parents who come to my workshops and I thank them for sharing.

Breastfeed, if possible, and do it for as long as you can. It has been shown that school children who were breastfed as infants have higher IQs. (Plus nursing is a great time to bond.) Whether or not you breastfeed, be sure you are looking the baby in the eyes when feeding them. Do not watch TV during feeding time. You do not want the baby to bond with the bottom of your chin!

Blow on the palms of the baby's hands. As you blow, say in a singsong chant; "here are Melissa's palms. I love Melissa so much." Repeat with other parts of the body. Most babies like gentle blowing on their elbows, fingers, neck, cheek and toes. Positive sensory interactions will advance cognitive abilities.

Gently massage her body as you smile into her eyes and say her name. The gentler the stimulation you give an infant, the greater the number of brain synapses and connections are formed.

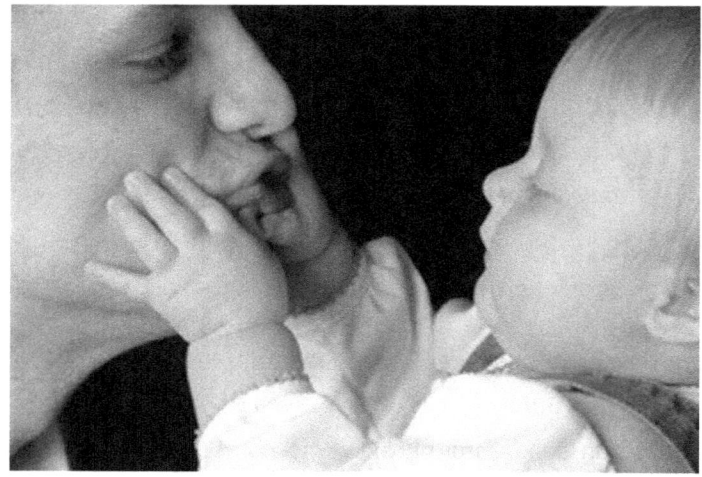

Lay your baby in your lap facing you. Extend your finger and watch her grab for it. Gently move your finger back and forth while you encourage her with "What a grip, you are so strong and brave." You are not only strengthening her hands and fingers, but also helping develop hand-eye coordination. This is also a good one to help with tracking skills.

Your infant may wake up many times during the night or take some quiet time before or after a nap. A mobile hung above the crib or by a nearby window will help make visual connections. The neurons for vision begin to form around two months.

"Turning the baby" game is a fun way to develop an awareness of space and a sense of balance. Exposing babies to different visual fields will develop hand/ eye coordination and balance, both of which are prerequisites for crawling and walking. As you turn with him in different directions, sing nursery rhymes.

Facial expressions are important to language development. Stare at your baby. When you are sure you have her attention, change expressions on your face. Frown, grimace, look excited etc.

Note: For the older child, my book, The Left Out Child: the Importance of Friendship, talks about the importance of reading body language. Many children do not recognize facial expressions or know how to interpret them. Help them by saying "This is how I look when I am worried" "This

is how I look when I am excited" Continue to work on recognizing facial clues with your child as they mature. When you see someone in a photo or newspaper, ask your children, "What do you think they are feeling? What does that expression mean to you?"

Talk, sing, talk, and sing over and over. The more you verbally interact with your baby the more her brain will make important connections needed for language. Talk about everything you are doing. Describe what you are doing, ask his opinion, discuss the weather or even carry on a one-sided debate over whether strained peas will be better than strained green beans. Just be vocal in introducing him to the wonderful world we live in.

Hug, kiss and cuddle. How we touch, treat and nurture infants can have a deep effect on the kind of adults they become. A child's capacity to control emotions hinges on early experiences and attachments.

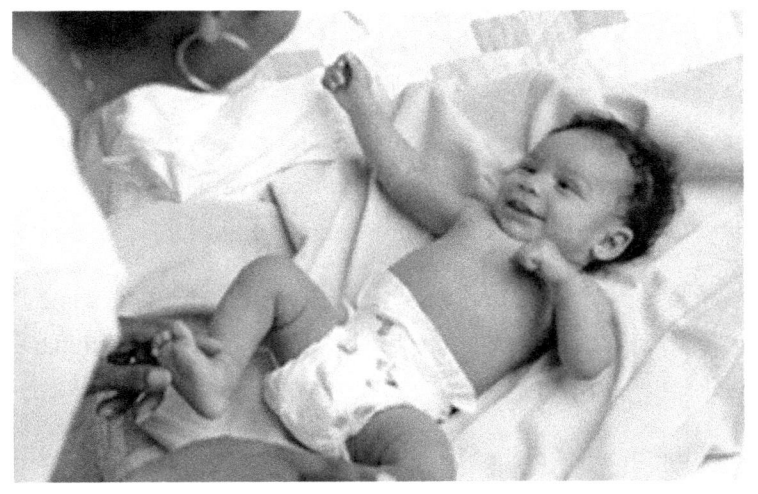

3 to 6 Months

At this age, your baby will begin to relax and enjoy himself, his caregivers, and the outside world. He will discover wonderful things to do with his voice and body language to communicate and connect with you. He will be clearer in his clues to let you know what he needs and when he needs it. He will also be more receptive to your verbal and non-verbal clues.

More ideas to make learning fun

Make eye contact and smile. Infants recognize your face and that of others who provide caregiving and love. Every time he stares at you, he is building up his memory.

Play classical music and sway to the beat. There is some research that suggests that listening to the rhythms of music is linked to learning math.

Make the most of diaper time. Ask permission to change his diaper. I know this sounds a little far reaching, but when visiting with my wonderful massage therapist, she taught me the concept of asking permission to touch the body of another. It ingrains a principal that your body is yours and no one should be touching it without permission. You will want to read more about this in my upcoming book *Caution Without Fear- Protecting Your Children From Sexual Abuse.* Look for it on www.ArtichokePress.com

Use the moments when you are dressing to teach the body parts or pieces of clothing. Help him to anticipate what will come next. Say "can you put your arm in the sleeve?'

You can help your little one to know and understand that buckling the car seat (or some other unpleasant or uncomfortable task) will not take forever. Say, "We are almost done. We just have to put the buckle in the slot. Can you hear the click?"

Use the mirror to teach visual concepts. Stand in front of the mirror holding your precious baby. Wave their hand and say, "Hello Ridge, how are you doing today? I like your red shirt." Pick up their foot and say, "Well hello foot, are you connected to Ridge?" Wave bye-bye and hello. Dance, prance and make faces in the mirror. You will both be giggling in no time.

Take walks and increase vocabulary. Put your baby in a front carrier, sling, or backpack and take a guided tour of the neighborhood. "Look at the red flower, can you see the brown puppy, now we are going past the bakery, can you smell the fresh bread?'

Exercising your baby's arms and legs will help develop his muscles and motor coordination. It also helps the brain refine the circuits for motor skill development. When he is lying on a firm surface, like a carpeted floor or a bed, hold his ankles and gently bend and straighten his legs. Sing or talk to him at the same time. Help him clap his hands and hold his arms above his head. It goes without saying, but I will say it anyway, if your baby resists, stop. Never force any movement.

Talk together. At this age babies often make lots of sounds. If her coos and gurgles are met with smiles and mimics of the sounds, she will want to repeat them because it makes you happy. If you answer your baby's cooing and then leave time for her to coo back, she will soon learn the pattern and rhythm of conversation.

Change the scenery. Move your baby's high chair or bouncer to another side of the room. This will challenge his memory of where things are as well as give new visual experiences.

Practice and model kind behavior. Say, "Please, thank you and excuse me" to your baby, spouse, extended family, grocer etc. When a child hears expressions of appreciation, he will learn that is the expectation of the family.

Play peek-a-boo. This age old game will do much more than make both you and your baby laugh and giggle. She will learn that objects can disappear and then come back.

Tell him what you are going to do before you do it. For instance, get in the habit of saying "I'm going to cover you with your red blanket." This will teach cause and effect. The number of words an infant hears each day will influence his future intelligence, social graces and ability to do well in school.

6 to 9 Months

This is a very exciting time for babies and those who care for them. This is when most babies will learn to sit alone, crawl, and pull to a standing position. These wonderful moments in history usually occur when there is no camera nearby.

This is a time when she will love to do a favorite activity over and over again. She wants to be included in social activities, even though she might be frightened of strangers. Allow her to be clingy when she needs it. This is normal and when she feels secure, she will be right back out there on the next great adventure. She will probably have started a wide variety of solid food and will have preferences, so be prepared.

More ideas to make learning fun

Take close-up pictures of all the important people in your child's life, make double prints and laminate them so they will not be harmed by chemicals in the photos. Lay them face up on the floor and help her find the two that are alike. As she grows older you will shuffle them around and face them down to help with memory. Another game is saying something like, "Where is the one who sings lullabies to you?" Show me the one who wears a hat?"

Because this a teething time, be prepared for everything to go in the mouth. That includes hands, feet, papers, rocks, dog, food etc. Have a good supply of teething rings and washable toys handy. Talk about what feels good to his teeth; "Does the silver ring feel good, how about the red rubber one?" Be empathic, so he knows you care even if you can't make it all better.

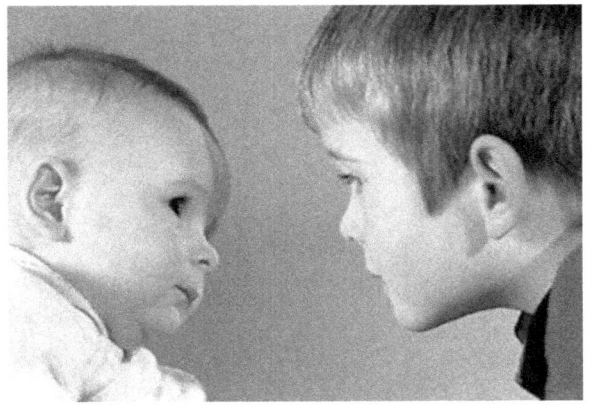

Develop auditory skills by using toys that make sounds. The more a toy responds to his handling with sound, change etc. the better it will be for developing cause and effect as well as eye hand skills.

Play show me your nose, eyes, ears, chin, fingers, tummy etc. Play where are my nose, eyes, ears, chin, fingers, and tummy etc. Now where is sister's nose, eyes, ears, chin, fingers, tummy etc.? Clap and smile when she gets it correct.

Play the same game with pictures in books or magazines. Show me the kitty. Show me the mommy. Show me the nose. Can you point to the horse? What do cows say? What do sheep say?

There is no need to buy expensive toys to teach auditory skills- just open your cupboard. There are many games you can teach your baby using your pots and pans. She will love putting the lid on and hiding things inside. You can hide small toys under an overturned pot and let her find them.

Hand her a wooden spoon, cover your ears and let her drum away.

When you read stories be sure to point to the different images and say the words over and over. "I see the kitty. Do you see the kitty? Where is the kitty?" You will be amazed at how quickly your little one can point to the image and recognize the word.

As soon as your baby can sit up easily, try rolling a ball to her. She will get very excited when she sees the ball coming towards her. Her motor dexterity is developing as she reaches and finally is able to catch and throw the ball.

Doing patte cake and peek-a-boo seem pretty tame, but they stimulate brain activity, communication skills, eye-hand and small motor skills. They also teach much about turn taking and prepare them for more intricate games later in life.

Puppets are wonderful teaching tools for children of all ages, but this age group especially loves them. Please don't feel you have to have professionally made puppets. A sock, mitten or corner of a blanket will do.

Tell stories using different voices and your baby will be entranced. It is important for the baby to hear the different tones and fluctuations of the voice in order to recognize different emotions.

To fine tune motor skills, fill a dishpan full of oatmeal and give the baby a measuring cup or two.

To learn about different textures, next time you have whip cream in a can, squirt some on the baby's high chair tray. Let him play, eat and have a ball. Be sure to get your camera ready.

On the next visit to the zoo, take photos of favorite animals to include in an album. Read it together, naming the animals and making the sounds.

Teach kindness by word and deed. Don't say, "Be kind to the kitty." Demonstrate what kindness is. "We are kind to the kitty, by brushing her fur this way."

This is a period when your baby responds to her own name. The baby will use their voice to express joy or displeasure. So talk and sing like never before because he is really focusing on the pitch and level of your voice.

9 to 12 Months

The word for this time is active, active, active. She will be able to get around by crawling and moving along furniture, and some children will take their first steps. Your child loves you and will become upset if you leave the room.

Crawling and walking are methods of getting into lots of things you had never even imagined he could find. At this age he has no concept of danger and very little memory of your warnings. Don't react to his investigation, but be proactive in childproofing your home.

It is hard to believe that what you do with your baby now will assist him in becoming a lifelong learner and especially a reader. But what you do now will make a big difference to the rest of his life.

He needs to learn many words and what they mean. Those who have a large vocabulary before they enter school have an easier time learning to read.

Even more ideas to make learning fun

Remember the photos you took to teach your child memory? Well, now is the time to help them develop a sense of humor and to grasp teasing in a gently way. Point to a picture of Aunt Debbie and say, "Is that Daddy?" Then laugh and tell her you were being silly.

Count everything. When you count out loud you are helping your child be aware of numbers, spaces and environment. So count your steps, his fingers, the blocks, the cows in the field or the pictures in the book.

Start giving choices to develop sense of self and confidence in decisions. Offer both a blue and red bowl for cereal in the morning. Let him choose between the banana and the apple slices for a snack.

Give the baby an opportunity to engage without you during interaction. Ask, "Do you want me to pick you up?" Extend your hands to her then ask again. Tell her "I am going to pick you up now, can you reach for me?

Use as many words as you can to say the same thing. For instance, "Wow, can you see the airplane in the sky? It looks little, but it is really far away."

Boost motor skills by building an obstacle course with pillows, toys and boxes. Teach her to go up, over, around and through. Congratulations are due for maneuvering the course. How about a hug and a kiss?

Want to know the best toy we ever found for an eight-month-old child? **Surprise.** It was a box of Kleenex. The first time she pulled them all out, I was annoyed. The second, third and subsequent times I realized what a fun game this was and how much more she loved it than the other high priced toys on the shelf and floor. Part of the fun, I am sure was my reaction!

Speaking of tissues, our daughter allowed her toddler son to see how far he could go through the house unrolling a roll of toilet tissue! They were counting, learning about corners, stairs etc. He loved it. She just learned to keep the bathroom door shut when she didn't want him to play that game anymore.

Equip your home with cushions and pillows and allow him to experiment with how to move around, over and with them all over the house.

Need I mention once again how important it is to sing, read and talk to your baby?

One to Two Years

Thank you so much for purchasing and reading this small book. The reason I write short books is because my adult daughters and all their friends with children tell me to. The parents I meet in my classes or in coaching ask me for more information.

They have given me the parameters of being small enough to:

- Fit in a diaper bag
- Or the side of car door
- Or the nightstand
- Or the back of the toilet
- Read in a half-hour
- Contain ideas that can be put into practice today
- Cost less than lunch at a fast food joint

They say they want simple, honest suggestions and tips from a real Mom and Dad. They don't like books written by doctors or psychologists who make them feel guilty. They want to know tips and techniques that have worked for other families, not just theory. So thanks again for sharing this time with us.

You will also want to join our community of kind, thoughtful people who want respect for all. Sign up to get a free eBook and notices of upcoming tele-seminars at http://www.judyhwright.com

Autism: Four Things To Watch For

While we have spend the last period talking about how you can enhance your relationship with your baby, now I want to share a reminder.

To our extended family, and us our precious baby may be the most beautiful, smartest and talented child ever to be born. However, sometimes it takes another pair of eyes and ears to see and hear things we may be missing in the development of our child.

It is important to be aware, but not afraid. You love your child more than any professional and if there is a situation that can assist his learning ability, you want to know about it. I trust you to find the most qualified help if you notice any red flags.

This is from my dear friend Dr. Patricia Nan Anderson in her book *"Parenting- A Field Guide"*(Aviva Publishing)

"Autism is an uncommon condition that interferes with children's ability to interact with other people. Since interacting with other people is what humans do, autism can create severe problems.

The good news is there are ways to help children with autism to function better. But the key is to start intervention early. Get a professional evaluation if you frequently notice these behaviors in your child:

1. He doesn't respond to his name. By the time a child is six months or so old, he should turn his had when you talk to him.

2. He doesn't look at what you want him to look at. By the time a child is eight months old or so, you should be able to point out a toy or doggie or something and have the child share this experience with you.

3. He doesn't' seem to pick up on other's emotions. Most eight-or-nine month old children will be sad if you are sad and happy when you are happy. If your child seen oblivious to other's feelings, that is a red flag.

4. He doesn't pretend. By the time a child is a year or eighteen months old, she should be able to understand that you are pretending when you hold a banana up to your ear and say "hello?" She should be able to "talk on the phone" with a pretend object by this time.

If you think there is a problem, check it out."

Remember, I am not a doctor, psychologist, or counselor. I am a Mom and a Gram who has worked with families for many years. It is my belief that we each learn and teach in a different way. Our autistic grandson teaches us every day.

We all have different abilities and the more we celebrate each individual the happier we all will be. Focus on the similarities and not the differences.

The Power of the Family

Nothing can quite prepare you for the 24/7 task of being a family, but you have my admiration and support for the most important job in the world. Family relationships are a basic need built into each of us.

The minute we add that small, demanding darling into our lives, our lives change forever more. Everyday situations take on new meaning and we look at the world with new eyes. Perhaps for the first time in our lives, we take a hard look at the future of the world and become concerned about what our lifestyle and the deeds of others are doing for the planet our little one is inheriting

One of the joys of parenting is that we can see growth and potential in our children and ourselves. As our children grow and develop, so do we. This sense of accomplishment sometimes gets lost in the day-to-day struggles and drama. Take a deep breath. You will find some amazing assistance at http://www.4lifehappykids.com/judy

Stop along the way to reflect on how much you and your child have grown and mastered skills that once seemed overwhelming. Don't get sucked into being a "perfect parent" because that is not a reality, even if you think your neighbor is one. Aim for 80% and it will be good enough. Our children have succeeded in spite of all the dumb things we did or didn't do. But they always knew they were loved unconditionally.

The next time you see a family, either one that is bound by blood or by choice, remember that such a group is the basic building block of society. They are a part of your village and you are a part of theirs. This is the place where the miracle of "us" happens.

The family plays the role of nurturing teachers, giving our children time, attention and direction.

Children need direction in the role as a life long learner. They are curious and filled with wonder and excitement at the world around them. If we, as caring adults can use our powers to guide them to know, love, feel, explore, choose and create we will be **Raising Smart & Kind Kids.**

Are you ready for the Toddler Years? Here they come, ready or not. Put on your racing shoes, because toddlers like to move quickly and all the emerging emotions are right there ready to be explored and shared at top volume.

Good luck and have fun with your toddler…

Raising Smart & Kind Kids:
The Toddler Years

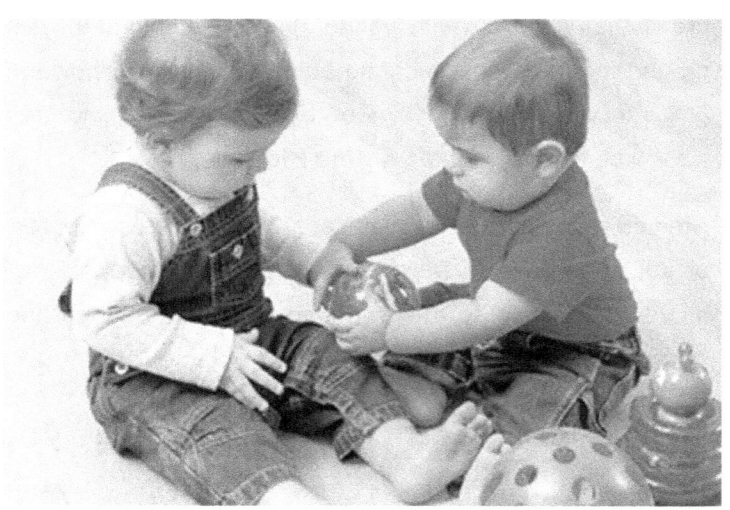

What is a Toddler?

Usually when children can walk on their own, they are called Toddlers. That frequently happens at one to two years of age, but some kids take their time learning to walk.

Just as a side note, it is vital that your child crawl to help his brain form patterns and later learns to read. If your little one went from sitting to walking, do some exercises to mimic leg crawls. Google **Brain Gym** for some family friendly exercises to increase all areas of the brain and body. Plus, they are just fun to do.

The Toddler stage is very important in a child's life. Everything that happens in this period is meaningful and they relate to the next stage of development. One major stage is to learn to be independent. Their verbal skills are not developed as yet and so they may become frustrated easily and you may become frustrated trying to determine what would make them happy.

Usually between 2 ½ and three years of age, children begin to take an interest in going to the toilet rather than wearing diapers. I have found girls to be somewhat easier than our son, but once again, each child is different.

These little budding geniuses are learning language and the power of the spoken word. They love to help around the house. I suggest you check out my book and training at www.KidsChoresAndMore.Com for a set of chores your toddler will enjoy doing to help make your house a home.

Toddlers are more active than at any other point in their lives, so keep them well fed nutritionally and well loved with nurture and understanding.

One of the best ways we found to train and teach our toddlers was with nursery rhymes. The patterns are great for early reading and Toddlers love to memorize and recite these short stories.

How is My Kid Smart?

Too many parents ask, "How smart is my kid?" when the real question should be, "how is my kid smart?" Every child is smart in his or her own way. Some children are physically agile while others are agile problem solvers.

Some youngsters will recognize a variety of emotions before they will recognize the letters of the alphabet. As your child grows and changes, your role as a parent stays essentially the same: to help children help themselves.

I'm happy to offer you some useful information and tips to help you raise smart, kind, creative and self-reliant kids.

We now know that while people are born with different brain configurations, the brain at birth is only accountable for about half your abilities. This brain matter your child inherited is really just *potential* abilities.

In order to really enhance the potential we need to have rich life experiences. Our DNA will only get us so far, it is the life experiences and life long learning that will develop the brain into a rich and rewarding intelligence.

Every Four Minutes

Research has shown that parents and caregivers of toddlers respond to their children at the rate of once every four minutes! If toddlers ask for attention at least once every four minutes, focus on what kind of attention you want to share. Rather than think of these interruptions as irritating, you will both be happier if you regroup your energy and treat these interruptions as "teaching moments."

Use these moments to assist with brain development and problem-solving skills, instead of correcting, criticizing or becoming angry.

ABC's of misbehavior

I like to think that when toddlers misbehave or act out they are really looking for one of these things:

- **Attention**—Look at me, see what I am doing. Tell me if I am doing it right. Help me know who I am and what kind of a person I am becoming.

- **Baby me**—I am not sure I am ready to learn all these new things. This is a transition time and I may bounce back and forth between independence and intra-dependence with my loved ones.

- **Cuddle me**—Help me feel secure and attached to you. I may resist your cuddles, but I still need them to reassure me of your unconditional love and forgiveness.

Behavior problems are necessary to learn life skills. It is important that parents, grandparents, childcare providers and teachers understand that behavior problems with toddlers are normal. It may not be fun to witness or take part in, but every toddler occasionally will have a "melt down."

Psychologists use the term "pre-abstract level of cognitive development" in relation to kids who are seven or younger. That fancy term means something different to us and to our child. To our child, it means, "I want what I want and I want it right now." A two-year-old's version of a clock has NOW stamped on it instead of numbers. To parents it means, "Can't you see I am fixing dinner and balancing the checkbook and trying to remember to bend at my knees, and I will get your ball in 3.5 minutes?"

Who is in Charge Here?

Remember pre-kid days when you could put your keys on the coffee table and they would still be there on Monday? Do you sometimes feel that you have little or no control over your house, sleep or life? Then welcome to living with a toddler.

Toddlers are incredibly self-centered. You will notice that your child can be happy, sad, angry and clingy all within a 15 minute time period.

Toddler years are especially challenging to the family when the child has an intensive personality. In private conversation between us as parents we referred to some of our children as "high maintenance." This is until we realized we were labeling and setting up expectations for them. But, if you feel that your child is a more demanding, high maintenance or intense kid than most, here are some tips that will make life easier for everyone involved:

- If your toddler is loud, use hand signals (we used hands over our ears) to indicate they were using an outside voice inside the house.

- Encourage lots of clapping, stomping and yelling games outside or for a timed period.

- Schedule lots of play dates in the park.

- Give distractible child lots of tasks or break down big jobs into little, short one.

- One of the ideas I suggested in **Kids, Chores & More,** is to draw a face on the belly with washable markers. When the socks are put away you draw one eye, when the shirts are put in the drawer another eye, when the pajamas are folded, it merits a nose. The mouth is the belly

button. Then your child does a wiggle dance to get the face to sing.

Emotional Development

During this period your child is learning how to behave around others. He will be more and more aware of pleasing you or displeasing you during the toddler years.

Somewhere around three, most children show such emotions as shame, embarrassment, pride, guilt or even envy. They are beginning to understand expectations, family rules and boundaries.

Emotions and Empathy

By the time a child is walking and talking somewhat, she begins to notice the emotions of others and respond to them. Your little one will be sad if you are sad and may try to comfort you.

Your little one will begin to identify their own feelings, name them and even notice that others have feelings too. Children as young as two or three value kind and fair treatment and have begun to understand that when they are unkind or selfish, others will not be happy with them.

I firmly believe that there is an envelope of time to demonstrate and model empathy and kindness. If it has not become a part of the inner guidance system (conscience) by the time the child is eight or nine, it will take adult intervention to teach kindness and empathy.

You don't have to teach character and heart values from scratch. It is my belief that we are hard wired to treat others with love, kindness and respect. Children who are able to see their important adults mentor and model these characteristics grow up knowing how to be a good person.

Discipline Yes-Punish No

Discipline comes from the root word "disciple" and means, "training to act in accordance with rules, instructions or learning, a regimen that develops or improves skills. This puts parents, grandparents, care providers who are in a position of authority with children in a role of leader and teacher who will train and encourage children to be good people, whereas to punish someone is to treat them harshly and to inflict a penalty for some implied offense or fault. One never learns from punishment, except to punish others.

As a friend's four-year-old child once said after receiving a spanking for an infraction "I can't wait till I'm big enough to hit someone." Needless to say, that was the last time they used corporal punishment.

Are You Listening to My Words?

If you get down on two-year-old Emma's eye level and tell her not to go into the street because she might get hurt, she will nod that she understands.

In fact, if you have told her ten times she may be able to repeat your words back verbatim. But she may still run into the street. "What?" you say. "How can that be?" The reality is that she may be unable to completely understand what you mean because her little brain is still developing.

Most preschoolers misbehave because they have not yet learned self-control. Sometimes we impose control on young children because it is easier and faster than trying to teach concepts and critical thinking.

Remember that our job as parents and loving adults is to teach our kids to help themselves. We want them to be able to think for themselves and make good decisions. So, please take the time to be consistent in teaching them skills they will need as a self-reliant adult.

QTIP and Toothpick

In my parenting classes, I always have QTIPs and toothpicks at each place. I never refer to them until the end of class, but everyone is curious about the meaning and importance of the items.

Finally, I share the meaning and ask the parents to carry them in their wallet or place them on their refrigerators to remind them of two very important concepts when dealing with children:

QTIP—Quit Taking It Personally Your child is learning and developing life skills and when she doesn't always do what you say, it is not a direct reflection on you as a parent.

Toothpick—Pick Your Battles Your job description is to help children to help themselves. Recognize that not all instructions will be obeyed, and not all conversations will be pleasant and it is okay to be grateful when they finally go to bed at night.

Rather than being frustrated when it takes a long time for your child to "get it," understand that you are teaching life-skills and once they do "get it," the lesson becomes an automatic action and a coping skill for life.

Quit Taking It Personally

It is not always about you.
Figure out who owns the problem.

Discipline the Deed (behavior)
Love the Doer (child)
Judy H. Wright, parent educator www.ArtichokePress.com

Knowing How to React to Misbehavior

A child needs to make sense of his world and figure out what is expected of him and that he is accepted. Even though you may want to encourage your child to have confidence and develop critical thinking, you may unknowingly send a message that says, "You are not enough as you are! I (the parent or teacher) will finally be happy when you reach your full potential."

As parents, we frequently put way too much pressure on our kids and ourselves. My husband Dwain and I have six adult children and ten grandkids. I love the honored place of being one generation away from temper tantrums and stubborn stances.

From a distance, I can clearly see the phases of a child's life. Grandmothers (and other older caring adults) know that misbehavior is not proof of a character flaw; it is part of growing up.

Tantrums, stubbornness and acting out offer kids opportunities to learn how to process their emotions, push physical boundaries and gain abilities.

Relax. This too shall pass.

Toddlers are busy becoming themselves. They often can't please themselves, let alone you. They have a hard time making up their mind and then they change it again and again.

Kids this age are naturally bossy and say no a lot. They insist on doing things their own way and become angry when they can't accomplish a task.

Your toddler is not being bad. She is becoming independent in the only way she knows how. Keep telling yourself things will be better soon.

Trust me. As a mom, grandmother, parent educator and wise woman- your child is going to succeed and be happy in life in spite of the mistakes you make as a parent. If you would like a quick report on specific self-soothing tips for parents check at http://amzn.to/kindlebyjudy

Firm and Kind

It is okay to insist on some limits of appropriate and acceptable behavior. You need to be both firm and kind when you step in to stop a situation from escalating.

Let your little one know it is okay to feel angry. But it is not okay to grab, bite, kick, or hit someone because she is angry.

Don't try to talk her out of unacceptable behavior. Just stop the action. Show clearly that you will not tolerate that behavior. Say "We do not hit others with toys" and remove the offending toy. Be prepared to listen to crying and screaming.

You can try distracting by offering another toy, but be consistent in your rules and limits. You are the adult and the teacher; he is learning how to behave from you.

Imagine Him Capable

When you have had it and are on the verge of turning in your membership to the parenthood association, take an adult break. Go somewhere quiet and take some deep breaths and picture your child in twenty years.

Visualize him across the desk from a corporate president interviewing for his first job after college. What kind of person do you want him to be?

What are the traits you want him to brag about? Then you can go back into the daily grind knowing that you are focusing on the end product.

Concentrate on the big picture and you won't be so overwhelmed by the little irritants. Now you have a game plan of what skills and values you want him to integrate into his life.

It is possible to be: smart and kind, self-reliant and responsible, honest and trustworthy, funny and respectful, courageous and competent, independent and empathetic. You can teach and model those characteristics every day.

Playing is Learning

Children love to play and play is their work. This is how they find out how the world works and who they are as a person.

They practice problem-solving skills and develop confidence as they conquer a formerly hard task.

Make learning fun

Learning is the byproduct of fun and togetherness. Your job as a parent is to influence, provide opportunity, encourage and participate, but not force. If you keep your focus on the fun - rather than on the grade or the test score -- you will raise a child who loves to learn. If your loved one has special needs, as does one of our grandsons with Autism, you will want to adapt some of the activities. I recommend that if you do have Autism in your family you check out http://judyhwright.com/autism for helpful resources. You will also find many learning activities and games in *Playful Parenting-Fun Games and Activities for Families available* at Amazon, http://amzn.to/kindlebyjudy.com and at http://www.ArtichokePress.com

65 Tips & Tricks To Raising Smart & Kind Toddlers

Develop your toddler's language, problem-solving and critical thinking skills, and emotional intelligence by using these ideas in daily life.

Language Skills

1. **Repetition:** Children must have the opportunity to practice a skill over and over, before it can become automatic action. Parents and caring adults need to understand that teaching involves many repetitions before something is learned and understood. This means kids will have to do things the wrong way *and* the right way many times before they learn to do it the right way consistently.

2. **Babbling is natural prelude to speech:** The age that your child acquires the ability to communicate is directly related to how much you interact by singing, talking and reading to her.

3. **Hearing and understanding language:** Your child will be able to understand many spoken words long before he acquires sufficient muscle skill to get his own lips and tongue around those words. Need I

preach the mantra again *Read, Sing and Talk* to your little one to raise a **Smart & Kind Kid**?

Toddlers are so active that sometimes they find it easier to substitute a movement for a word. They will run around the room with their arms flapping to indicate flying rather than saying the words.

Speaking in Sentences: As your child's speech improves and his vocabulary grows, he will begin to form short sentences. *No more. More please. All gone.* Language will usually progress to three word sentences; *Where Mommy at? Why Sammy sad?* And then eventually into correct simple sentences. Many boys, for some reason, are slower to form sentences than girls, and are perfectly content to mumble and point.

This mumbling and pointing condition arises again when your teenage son is perfectly capable of communicating; he just make the choice not to do so to annoy his parents.

A Word A Day: How quickly will your child's vocabulary grow? It depends on you, your child, the word and a thousand other variables. Try one new word a day. If you use the word in sentences, tell him the meaning and then repeat it throughout the day. It will become part of the speech pattern. Don't think that he will not comprehend the meaning even if he can't say all the words. Ask him if he understands the meaning or can think of when you would use the word.

Learning Letters: Pre-reading skills come from recognizing letters and words. Always point out and read frequently seen signs, such as STOP, NO EXIT, and YIELD. Look for letters that are used in your child's name.

Word Play: Vocabulary is one of the best indicators of school success, so talk, read and sing with your toddler a lot. If you are stuck in traffic or in a waiting room play the word game of opposites. This is fun for kids to learn the opposite of up is down. Now try fast, happy, big, tall, stand, asleep, etc. As they get older make the words more complicated. You will be surprised at how this will increase their vocabulary and understanding of language.

Grow a Vocabulary. Teach your child the nouns of words first; that is the names of things he sees often in his daily life, for instance: car, glass, spoon. Say *bath* several times before placing him in the bath. Say *spoon and bowl.* The child will begin to recognize the words in a context that is understandable and this is a foundation for learning to read.

As your toddler gains a listening vocabulary, parent's conversations begin to make sense. This skill of learning to listen will help as your child hears you read stories. Ask him to point to the spoon in the story, the spoon on the table, the spoon in the sandbox.

Letter Find: As you read the Sunday paper together, give the child a section you have finished and a highlighter pen. Challenge him to find 10 A's and then 10 B's etc. Perhaps he can spell out his name by looking for the letters.

Make ABC cookies: Make your favorite sugar cookie recipe (or buy a roll from the grocery store—this is not about Parent's Magazine Mommy of the Year) and roll it into a flat surfaces and cut into long strips. Have your little one make animal shapes, alphabet or monsters. It is a fun way to teach the alphabet to the kids and after they are baked, it is even more fun to eat them.

Talk, Read and Sing: Talk about everything. Ask questions. Explain how things work. Make your conversations pleasant and fun. Actually listen to what your child is telling you and create a dialog. Reading aloud at least 20 minutes a day will increase your child's comprehension, vocabulary and communication skills.

Plus, it is just plain fun to snuggle up with your toddler as long as you can. Soon they will be grown and reading to their own children. We recommend <u>Highlights Magazine</u> for age-appropriate, fun reading.

Story People: Use the refrigerator to post pictures of faces and activities and ask the toddler to "tell you the story." What do you think is happening? What do you suppose they are thinking? What do you think will happen next? What would You do if that were you?

Parts of The Body: Does your toddler know the different names for the parts of his body? Ask him what we call this part and to point to it on a doll or on you. Don't forget the knuckles and eyelashes.

How Did It Get Here? Go through the house and tell the story of how you obtained the furniture and accessories. Our grandson Justus has a favorite story of a ring with many stones and he has named all the stones for various family members and pets.

Children's Museums: Sometimes we adults find it hard to focus on playing with our children when there are so many grown-up distractions at home – bills to pay, laundry to fold, dishes to wash, etc.
Many communities (both small towns and big cities) now have children's museums where parents and kids can interact and play without all of those distractions. If your budget allows, buy a membership or annual pass so that you can visit the children's museum as often as you like.

Answer Questions: If you don't know the answer then be very open about not knowing and be willing to find out. By doing this, you are encouraging your child to be a problem-solver.

Keep a running list of questions you want to find answers for and then take your child and the list to the library. One of the families that were in my classes did not have the resources for computers, but would make a trip to the library weekly to find answers.

She said the librarian loved to see the whole family come in and actually started calling them the "Stump The Librarian Group."

Help Them Figure Out Solutions: Remember, for every situation there is at least five solutions. But with toddlers, work with three at the most. So, when they come to you with a problem help them to find different solutions.

Ask them what will happen if they choose this solution, then ask, "What else could we do to solve the problem?"

As you assist them in developing cause and effect thinking, they will realize that for every action, there is a reaction.

You do realize that even when you teach this method to a toddler, you will have to revisit the lessons when they reach their teen years.

Importance of Good Language Skills: Language skills include the ability to be fluent and readily understood in the common language of the culture where you live.

If your child speaks a language other than English and lives in an English predominant speaking culture, make sure your child speaks and understands English at a very early age.

This is also true if you are an English–speaking child living among non-English speakers. Don't let your child be misunderstood or lack friends because of speech problems.

Speech Problems: At some point most children need some speech therapy! Yes, that is what you are doing when you teach them to say things in a certain way, or to pronounce words correctly.

However, if you child continues to have problems pronouncing words or saying certain parts of speech, then you may want to consult a professional.

Don't assume your child will outgrow a speech problem. That may not happen. Besides, it just gives mean kids ammunition to tease and taunt, when it can be corrected easily.

Hearing Words: We just assumed our son was a little stubborn when he was asked to do small chores. When I took him to a pre-school checkup I was mortified that he had a hearing loss. Yes, once again, had to disqualify myself from "Mother of the Year Award."

Fortunately, it was enlarged tonsils and adenoids and it was affecting his hearing. He came out of the operating room so excited because he could hear a baby crying down the hall.

Some kids will manifest hearing loss with lots of earaches or ear infections. He has a high pain level and had never complained. (That pain tolerance has served him well in soccer, skiing and other extreme sports.)

Using Kind Words: As a parent or loving adult, you will need to edit some of your child's language. They will learn vocabulary from peers, television and on the street that you may not want them to use.

Kids love to try out the sounds of new words. They like to see the reaction they get from you. Some of the words they use will be curse words. Some will be slang words. But some will be racist or bigoted words.

These children are being born in a global economy and playground. They cannot afford to be bigoted, racist or any other form of hateful mind-set. It is imperative that they have respect for all.

It is your responsibility to say, "We don't use that kind of language." Or, "That is a very unkind word and it is not allowed at any time." Or "When people use that word they are saying something very mean about another person. We are not like that. We respect other people and treat them with kindness."

Otherwise, your child will assume that the word is an acceptable one.

Good Language Builds Self Esteem: A child who has learned good communication skills will also gain confidence that he or she can communicate well with others. He or she will fit in more easily with all kinds of people and will be able to share and experience their contributions.

Good language skills do not automatically build self-esteem, but bad language can bring about the rejection and teasing that will destroy self-esteem.

One of the characteristics of individuals with good self-esteem (see ArtichokePress.com for book "Building Self Confidence With Encouraging Words) is being communicative. Which simply means that people with high confidence know how to ask for what they want and to speak up in social situations.

Problem-solving and Critical Thinking Skills

- **Build Problem Solving Skills:** Children who have learned to face problems as they occur and to try to solve those situations usually think of the world as a fair place. This is such a powerful life skill and we often think of it in regards to the workplace, but it is a learned behavior from childhood.

Steps to solving a problem

- **First define the problem.** "You want the round piece of the toy to fit in the square space."

- **Name as many feasible solutions as possible.** " Would the round piece fit here in the triangle? How about trying the oblong shape? What happens if you try it in the rectangle shape hole?

- **Choose the solution that has the best outcomes.** Avoid jumping in and solving the problem for your toddler. Remember, your job is to help your child help himself.

- **One, Two, Buckle My Shoe:** Nursery rhymes are an essential part of learning. The rhythm and beat of the words helps your child to learn patterns of language.

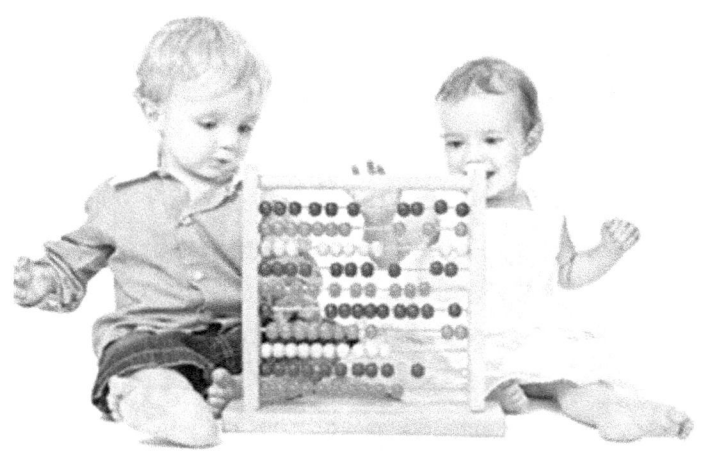

- **Counting and Comparing:** Teach the concept of one and two with objects, like spoons or blocks. Then you extend to three and four and more. It is fun to teach kids to count to 100 but it really doesn't mean as much unless they can grasp that 100 is more than just a bunch of words to memorize. Help them to find four red toys, then five sticks and then six rocks. Help them to understand more and less, bigger and smaller, shorter and taller, light and heavy.

- **Sequencing- What Comes Next?** Find or draw three pictures of a child on a trike, falling off, and the mom putting a band aide on the scratch. Ask your toddler to put them in order. Or just find a picture in a magazine of a child on a trike. (Example—you can use any picture) ask your toddler what does the child do before he gets on the trike. What does he have to do to make the trike move? Where does he put his feet, hands and body?

- **Corrective Feedback and Positive Reinforcement:** When your toddler is being impossible, try saying to him, "Buddy, I am getting very upset by the screaming. I can't understand what you need and you must calm down and tell me why you are so upset."

If he can calm down by himself, problem solved. Children don't usually want their parents to be mad at them. If he continues to scream then pick him up and hold him closely but firmly on your lap. Some parents have a soft blanket to wrap up his body. Say, "Since you are having trouble controlling yourself right now, I am going to control you until you can calm down."

A good follow-up is a kiss and hugs to make both of you feel better. Once the toddler has become calm enough to use words, discuss what he needed and why his behavior made you angry. He didn't make you angry. You were angry over the behavior.

- **Fix It, Don't Just Forget It:** A big part of child's self-esteem is the ability to know what to do in emergency situations. This is a big part of teaching problem solving skills

We want our kids to be prepared for emergencies and for recognizing that we all have limited resources and so we need to salvage what is good. Sometimes that means a relationship, a pair of jeans or a broken toy.

How do you teach this to your child? First, you admit that you can't teach every single correct response to every single situation.

Your responsibility is to teach your child how to get answers.

The library or Internet can teach you and your child so much, but then so can the manuals that come with toys. Help your child to see the sequence of solving problems by breaking a problem down into logical steps.

Benefits of finding answers and following instructions are that the child learns how to repair or re-engineer different parts and pieces. This teaches that her that not everything is disposable just because it is no longer in optimum condition.

I know it seems a little bit of a stretch to understand this at first, but it is important for your child to see you model how to repair or improve a broken object or difficult situation. This helps them to understand that we don't just give up on things that are not working just right.

- **Outside Time Out:** When I heard Chris Ober, one of the authors of **Earthing,** speak, it really resonated with me. So often humans feel disconnected from the earth and need to be grounded to the natural patterns of life.

When your toddler needs a time out to re-group her little feelings, body and attitude, how about a time out spent with feet on the ground and surrounded by nature? She will recover her emotional balance in rhythm with the earth's vibrations, rather than sitting on a chair wondering what it was that made Dad mad now?

- **Shapes and Sizes**: Make a puzzle by drawing around cookie cutters with a fine line Magic Marker on a big sheet of plastic or cardboard. Have your toddler match the drawings with the shapes. After she has done it a few times, turn the paper sideways. Then do another with even smaller pieces with unusual shapes.

- **Smells and Aromas:** Take four or five plastic dishes and add various foods with distinctive smells. When we did this, we had cinnamon in one bowl, peanut butter in another, pepper in another, rose petals, oatmeal etc.

After your toddler gets familiar with the smells, have him close his eyes. Hold the bowl under his nose and see if he can identify the smell. Throw in an empty one to surprise him!

Teach him about the power of aroma and what smells bring back what memories to you. Mine is Lilacs and family picnics at my grandparents. What smells trigger-happy memories for you?

When you go outside, teach your toddler to inhale deeply and try to determine what he smells. Is it flowers, a charcoal grill, dog poop, fresh cut grass etc.

- **The Kitchen Drawer:** Set aside one drawer to fill with pans, wooden spoons, measuring cups to nest, old spice bottles filled with noise makers (make sure lids are on tight), egg beaters, and any other wonderful equipment to make a pretend dinner while you are busy.

- **Build a Gallery of Art Projects:** When we want to show how much we value a child is to display and support their artistic endeavors.

Show that you believe the work they are doing is important. Much o your toddler's artwork isn't going to make any sense to you. It may not look pretty. You may not even have a clue about what it is supposed to be. So ask them.

When you encourage your child to express their creativity they then feel more confident in doing more. It is almost as if they think, "Hmm, if mom and dad like my picture of colors, maybe they will like my dance or my song."

93

Express your appreciation for the effort, skill and perseverance that your child has put into projects. If your child gives you art, then display it prominently.

- **Beautiful Oops**: Get out paper and paints and have your little one spill on purpose. You can then use crayons or markers to turn the random shape of the spill into something remarkable – a mountain in a landscape, a mythical creature, or a continent on a newly discovered planet.

- **Textures and Treasures**. Create a treasure box full of all different textures for your toddler to explore. When you are on a walk and find a bird feather say "Wow, a feather. Feel how soft it is, but it has a hard part too. Shall we take this home to put in our treasure box?"

Spend some time discussing the various materials in your box. Are some things bumpy, hard, smooth, stretchy or see-through? This is such a great tool for teaching and *surprise!* It doesn't cost anything and it is not found in a toy store.

When you are using words to describe textures, you are sharing information that will help him understand many other things in life.

I dare you to describe with just words what corduroy is. You really have to feel it to grasp the concept.

Have your little one share this treasure box with a grandparent or loving Auntie. The true learning comes from the teaching, and toddlers have so much to teach us.

- **Science Skills:** The most mundane thing to an adult is a learning adventure to a toddler. As you are on a walk and finding leaves, take the few extra minutes to explain how trees grow and that the root system is probably the same size as the part they can see. Examine a piece of the bark with your handy-dandy magnifying glass. Pretty neat patterns to see and maybe even copy on paper? Ask your child what to do.

- **Invention and Design:** Where do the toys we play with and the clothes we wear come from? It all starts with an idea in someone's head. Show how finding new ideas is important and encourage him to think of new ways to do things.

- **Guide, Don't Push:** If your child gets frustrated because he cannot make the shapes fit in the box, encourage her to try again, and then put your hand over hers and softly guide it. That way she will learn, but will still feel that she has done it correctly.

- **Run and Play:** Kicking a ball around outside is not just a way to get rid of excess energy; it is a means of learning physical coordination, motor skills and bonding with a parent or teacher.

- **Create with Spaghetti:** When you cook spaghetti, or raiment noodles give your toddler a few strands on a placemat and ask if she can make shapes with it. This is just another activity with pasta. There are so many lessons to be learned from such a staple in our diet.

- **Music and Dance:** Hold your toddler in your arms, standing with her feet on top of your feet or kneel down so you are closer in size. Now dance to the beat of her favorite song.

-

Pick the Winner: Put three of your toddler's favorite toys on a chair. Hold each one in your hand and say the name and the color (or function – "has wheels"). Then name one of the toys and ask him to hand it to you. When he picks the right one, clap and giggle. Make it fun; it is not a test. Doing it correctly will result in a good feeling, not an automatic entry into Harvard.

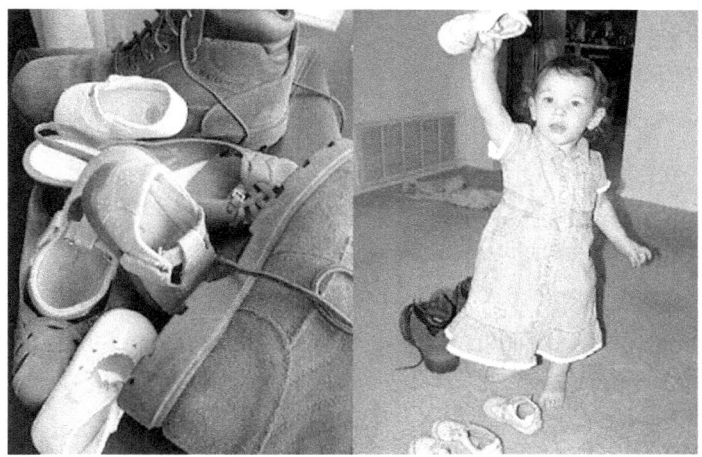

- **Matching Shoes:** This is such a fun game, and you can clean out the bottom of your closet while you are at it. Put the left shoes in a pile in the hall. Put the right shoes in a pile in the corner of the bedroom. Ask the toddler to find the matches. Be sure to talk about something on the shoe to help her understand why they go together; blue color, tassel, gold heel, etc.

- **Macaroni Necklaces.** Just like the appearance of exercise equipment makes a yard sale official, macaroni necklaces make love official. You can dye the macaroni with a little food coloring and then give the kids a long string of yarn. Tape the end and it will make stringing easier. Be sure to tie one piece of macaroni crosswise so the other ones don't fall off the end. Wear it with pride; it was made with love.

Body Awareness: Here is a favorite of my children and grandchildren. Moving your finger in a circle, say very quietly, "From the barn to the house, comes a little brown mouse to take a bite of your...belly, nose, toe, hand, elbow etc." This gentle tickling and chasing game is fun as the children try to anticipate where the mouse will want a bite.

House Rules: Children who live without some boundaries tend to be anxious and insecure because they don't know what to expect.

Set family or house rules in terms of what you DO want your children to accomplish rather than what you DON'T want to happen. When rules are stated as "In our house we only eat food at the table" it is in force no matter who is in charge; parents, grandparents, babysitters or friends.

- **Role Models:** Young children like to imitate adults, so buy sturdy small wheelbarrows, brooms and rakes.

- **Chores:** Even a Toddler wants to help make the house a home and is ready to learn responsibility. To find a selection of realistic expectations of each age and stage, go to one of my most popular books and workshops http://www.KidsChoresAndMore.com

Choices, Choices: When you are shopping, allow your toddler to decide which item to buy by giving him a choice between two acceptable options. Help him understand the prices, size differences and how the product will be used.

This is a basis for critical thinking, which will serve him well in any occupation or career he may chose. Speaking of choices, my friends and I love to shop at http://www.judyhwright.com/gigglebaby for the little ones in our lives.

Yellow Day: Let your child plan a "yellow day" or a "red day" where you wear red eats red and look for red in the neighborhood.

What a Wonderful World: Ask friends and relatives to send postcards representative of where they are living or visiting. Have them describe the natural wonders of that area, along with their interpretation of customs, cultures and places to visit. Your child can collect them in a special box (perhaps a shoe box). As he gets older, he can find them on a map and maybe plan a trip!

Reasons to Recycle: Encouraging a preschooler to understand the environment and to see that we all have a responsibility to the earth is easy. Perhaps he can be in charge of dumping vegetable scraps in the outdoor compost pail. Or picking up litter. Explain why we do this to help the earth.

I Spy With My Little Eye: A wonderful investment from the dollar store is a big magnifying glass. Look at all sorts of things inside and out. Really look. How long has it been since you have examined a leaf in such detail? Isn't nature wonderful?

Creative Messes and Imagination: In order to have a child who is inquisitive and full of courage, we must understand that it is messy some times. Our children loved to make forts and tunnels out of sofa cushions. Our grandsons build an elaborate maze with canned vegetables, boxes and masking tape that extended down a flight of stairs and had many false endings. It took them all day to build it and me a long time to figure it out.

- **Food Origins:** To a toddler, butter comes in a box and you put it on toast. Talk about the industry involved in gathering the ingredients, cooking them and shipping the final product to your store.

Visit a farmer's market to introduce your youngster to food makers in their own community. Help your child develop a love of eating good food by cooking; shopping and growing your own produce from the garden you have planted together.

Help him to appreciate the long-term effects of shipping foods over long distances and the value of eating locally grown food as much as possible. This will help him see himself in a global context.

- **Artistic Expression:** Small rollers made for painting trim are wonderful tools of imagination for toddlers. You can buy them at a hardware store or most dollar stores. Just give your little artist a bucket of water and let them paint the sidewalk, porch or deck.

- **Cardboard Castles:** Ask the appliance store if they could save a couple of large boxes for you. These boxes of imagination can be a castle one day, a boat another and a stage for a play performed with sock puppets.

- **Water Play:** Toddlers love to play in suds and water. Why not let them wash the dishes or silverware? Do it together and have fun. They learn patterning and sorting by putting clean silverware in the drawer or dirty silverware in the dishwasher. See http://www.kidschoresandmore.com for more suggestions of realistic expectations for the ages and stages of the child.

- **Measure It Out:** Instead of buying an expensive toy at the toy store, buy a bunch of measuring utensils at the dollar store. At bath time, encourage your toddler to measure how many teaspoons of water will go into the ½-measuring cup.

How many cups does it take to fill the one-quart pitcher? This exercise teaches cause and effect, early math, opposites (empty-full, big-small) and it is just plain fun to play in water. Often when kids are cranky, a warm bath will sooth their ruffled feathers and calm down tempers-theirs and yours.

- **Finger Paint with Food**: Give your artist a special place mat and tell her that she can draw something great and eat it too. We have used chocolate pudding, but a class participant said her son especially loved the whipped cream in a can that was left over after pumpkin pie.

- **Following Directions**: Give one short direction like touch your nose. Then add another more complicated one- touch your nose and jump three times. Then another one- touch your nose, jump three times, then clap your hands.

- **My Life Story**: Next time you are at the computer, ask your child to tell you a story about their life. Type it up and let them color pictures. Or you can add pictures from your computer. Be sure to keep it. We treasure the ones our kids did when they were 6, 12 and 18.

- **Dress Up and Dream On**: Keep a box of hats, jewelry and clothing that can be used in playing "let's pretend." Watch for wonderful costumes at yard sales to keep in the dress up box.

Emotional Intelligence

- **Find the Feelings:** Use a game like *Feeleez* or flip through the pages of a magazine to help your child develop empathy. By pointing out pictures of people who are happy, surprised, angry, sad, and thoughtful, etc., you are helping your child develop a vocabulary of emotions.

After they have learned these new words for feelings, ask them to show you a sad face, or an angry face. A well-developed sense of empathy will be extremely helpful as they begin to navigate the world of friends and classmates.

- **Discipline without Damage:** The word discipline has roots in the word disciple. It means to guide, lead, teach and mentor. It does not mean to punish. Punishment is harsh and creates resentment and ill will.

Discipline is kind, fair, consistent and done in a way that will not harm the physical, emotional or spiritual well being of your child. Remember, it is the behavior that is irritating you, not the child. Separate the two.

- **Turn off the Television and Electronic Games:** There is so much to do outside and inside to stimulate the imagination and get body and brain cells moving. I really recommend you limit the time spent in front of electronic baby sitters.

Kids need ideas and they can come up with great activities and play games. Even the best of educational games is a "one size fits all" and your child is unique.

- **Smile:** Are you aware that the human body is not capable of holding a negative thought when you smile? If your little one wakes up grouchy or with a frown on her face give her a hand mirror and ask her just to smile while you set the timer for however many minutes as she is old.

- **Make Time Real Time:** Telling your toddler you will do something tomorrow is an exercise in futility. Then they will bug you with "Is today tomorrow or is it yesterday?" Help them chunk periods of time in a relevant way for them to understand. "We will go after lunch." "It will take about as long to do as it takes us to get dressed." "You brush your teeth while I sing happy birthday twice. That is how long you are supposed to brush."

- **Don't Compare:** Your child is not the same as her friends, cousins, siblings or other playmates. Each child follows a unique timetable of learning and has a different set of interests.

- **Yell Less, Tell More:** Young children have difficulty remembering long strings of verbal words. Make your sentences and instructions short and clear.

Speak in a clear, calm voice. Only scream if the house is on fire or there is a bear in the living room.

- **Comment on Character Traits.** Equally as important, or perhaps more important, than being smart is the ability to be kind. Formation of a child's character and values are best installed in the heart of the young child.

Be sure to share positive comments when your child shares his toys. Remark on his bravery when he tried a task that frightened him before. Make note when he is kind to a neighbor or an animal.

Rather than commenting on the act by saying something like, "good job," comment on the character or heart trait by saying something like, "That was a thoughtful thing for you to do. It makes me happy to see you more understanding of how others feel."

- **Get Curious, Not Furious:** Instead of immediately jumping to the conclusion that your toddler is misbehaving or determined to drive you crazy, ask some questions. Many times just asking, "What do you need?" is sufficient. Maybe try, "Why are you frustrated? What can I do to help you find a solution to your unhappiness?"

- **Listen to Your Heart.** We are all born with an intuition of knowing what is best for us. Help your child to develop this inner voice and to reaffirm positive thoughts. If he says, "Oh I am so stupid." Stop the conversation and have him change the wording to something like, "Sometimes I make dumb choices, but usually I am pretty smart about things. Next time I will choose differently."

- **Listen to Your Gut:** Help your child (and yourself) to pay attention to the feelings you get that something is not right. Help them to be aware but not afraid of surroundings, situations and certain people. If your child tells you he doesn't like or trust someone, believe him.

- **Catch Them Doing Good:** for everything a child does wrong, he does 19 things right. Children who only receive attention when they have misbehaved or made poor judgments soon learn to blame others and avoid responsibility.

- **I Feel Method:** Find a time when you are really happy to be her parent and tell her using the "*I feel method.*" I feel so proud of you when I see how kind you are to Grandma." " "I feel so happy when I see you and your brother playing so well together."

Studies show that it takes 13 positive statements to counteract the effect of a negative statement. If you make a point of expressing positive feelings at least twice as often as you do negative one, you will be on the road to good family communication and a more confident, loving child.

- **Encourage Positive Action:** Point out what you do want, rather than what you don't want. Try to motivate rather than intimidate for good behavior. Say, "The toys go in the box," or, "I want you to hold my hand." You will enjoy a free eBook on this subject at http://www.UseEncouragingWords.com. This is my gift to you and your children.

- **Teach Diversity and Appreciate Abilities**: Between the ages of two and five, children notice and make comments about why others are different than them. They can be uncomfortable or curious about someone who is different than them. This is your opportunity to teach empathy, openness and kindness

Listen carefully and talk openly and honestly about differences with others. If your child stares at someone in a wheelchair, say in a matter-of-fact way, "His legs don't work the same as yours, so he uses his wheelchair to go from place to place."

Teach Without Anger, Shame or Blame

The messages, values and standards they receive from you will affect how they think and feel not only about themselves, but the world around them.

All parents get angry sometimes. Even caring ones or your child's friend's parents who do everything right according to your child. However, when we are angry, old thought patterns come rolling around in our brain and we react in ways we ordinarily would not do.

Not only do hurtful words strike the heart of the child but also the *inference* of what he thinks we mean. So when a glass of milk is spilled and the parent yells "How could you be so clumsy? Milk costs a lot of money and now I have to drop what I was going to do and run to the store to have milk enough for breakfast. The child not only hears the words but feels the message that he is a:

1. Clumsy person
2. He is costing the family money they don't have
3. It is his fault that his mother is tired and has to run to the store
4. Because of his actions, the whole family is suffering.

When in reality, a 20-cent glass of milk was spilled. The family would need more milk soon anyway. The family lost 20 cents in milk but the child lost a great deal of confidence.

How much better it would have been for Mother to say, "I see the milk is spilled. Here is a sponge."

When things go wrong it is not the right time to try to correct personality flaws or make the child feel worse than he already does.

Just deal with the event, not the person. The key thing to remember about shame and guilt is that the action may have been a mistake, but the child never is.

Encourage them to be smart and kind by you being a smart and kind example for them to emulate.

Children Learn What They Live

If a child lives with criticism,
He learns to condemn.

If a child lives with hostility,
He learns to fight.

If a child lives with ridicule,
He learns to be shy.

If a child lives with shame,
He learns to feel guilty.

If a child lives with tolerance,
He learns to be patient.

If a child lives with encouragement,
He learns confidence.

If a child lives with praise,
He learns to appreciate.

If a child lives with fairness,
He learns justice.

If a child lives with security,
He learns to have faith.

If a child lives with approval,
He learns to like himself.

If a child lives with acceptance and friendship,
He learns to find love in the world.

~ Dorothy Law Nolte, Ph.D.

Final Notes on Toddlers

It is probably difficult for you to believe how quickly your little baby has grown into this independent individual with very distinct tastes and opinions. Remember your job, as a parent is to help children help themselves.

As a caring adult, I am excited about the future of the world. It is because I have seen and worked with the loving parents and their amazing children who will find new and ingenious ways to solve problems.

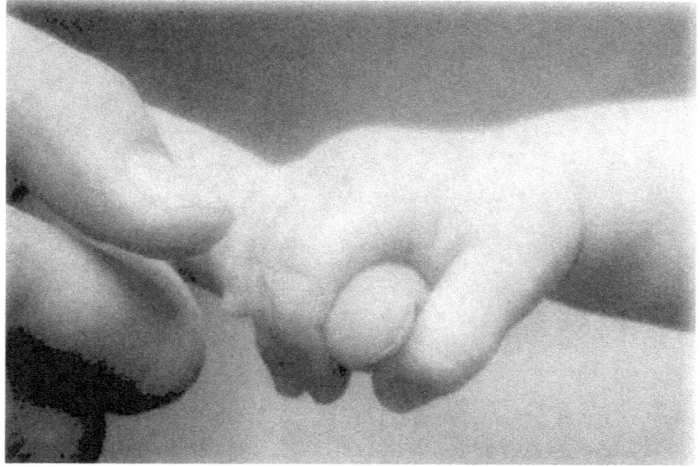

Our world is in good hands with caring adults and smart and kind kids.

Thank you so much for doing this important work of modeling and mentoring the next generation.

Are you ready for Preschool Years? Here they come, ready or not. ...

Raising Smart & Kind Kids:
The Preschool Years

What Are The Rules In Life?

This is the age when children clearly move from playing along side each other to playing with each other. This is also a time of endless questions; when? Why? How? What if? How come? Why not? Why? Why?

What make it possible for 3 to 6 year old kids to navigate the world of school, friends, and life are their understanding of how things work and "the rules of life." This is the period when the best teaching is done with logical and natural consequences, rather than lecture or shaming.

Teasing or ridicule by adults or peer group is particularly damaging at this age, because they are trying so hard to know what to do. Too much harshness can cause a child to withdraw and become discouraged.

Critical thinking comes when your child can figure it out for himself with some help from loving adults. For instance, "If I share my toys with him, he will be my friend."(Logical consequence) If I don't put my trike in the garage, it may get stolen and then I won't be able to ride it." (Natural consequence.)

The Confident Learner

There is no single key to academic success, but there are several ways you can improve your child's chances of enjoying a lifetime of learning. You can establish a home atmosphere that encourages a child to learn and to enjoy school. The more you can instill confidence and co-operation, the easier your child will navigate the system of education.

Children and adults who have strong relationships with significant people in their circle know they belong to a tribe, family or community. They have a confidence that shows in their physical demeanor as well as their courage to be open to opportunities.

Attachment and connected parenting has a positive influence on how kids will turn out. When a baby's cues are read and her needs taken care of, she learns to trust her caregivers and her environment. As the child grows and develops they have a foundation of security and safety.

Research (and my own observations) found that preschoolers who have a connected background make friends more easily. They are also more flexible and yet able to hold their own against aggressive children on the playground.

This confident self-assurance has very little, if anything, to do with status, education, employment or culture. Adults who succeed in teaching children to think for themselves generally value freedom to think in creative ways and convey a joy of learning for learning's sake. Some of these adults may be highly educated and earn lots of money, but most are just good, happy citizens who value their skills and enjoy their lives. Their confidence is contagious to a new generation of learners.

The Kind and Capable Learner

Caring adults bring a sense of fun, wonder and adventure to learning. These individuals recognize and model being both capable and kind. They enjoy exposing the child to the wonderful world, to opportunities that are created in each day and to those opportunities yet to come. They believe in the basic goodness of all people. Caring adults share an example of seeing the human as well as the spiritual in all people and cultures.

They show respect and understanding for all kinds of learning, not just book learning. They show respect for all kinds of people, not just those who are intellectually equal to them. They understand the *difference between knowledge and wisdom.* A true teacher or mentor desires wisdom and understanding for themselves and the ones with whom they share their knowledge.

One of the most important qualities I see in those parents, coaches, teachers and child-care providers that positively influence the learning abilities in those they work with: *They see students as individuals, not just as minds to be taught with facts. They see each person as individual and unique. They seek a mutually respectful relationship with each individual, which accepts and values individual talents and skills.*

It sounds so basic, but it is true. To create a kind and capable learner, a teacher must model kindness and show an appreciation for the capabilities of each student.

The Confident, Kind and Capable Teacher

You are that teacher. You have a calling to prepare your child -- and the children you influence -- to engage in the most exciting time in the history of the world. Your child has no idea what he will be when he grows up, because it has not been invented yet.

Hopefully, you can assist her to have the confidence, courage, critical thinking and problem solving skills that will allow her to invent the career, widget or program that will make this world a better place.

As a worldwide community, we want those leaders and inventors to come from homes filled with wonder, love and respect. We want them to take the opportunity to create from a foundation of love and acceptance.

When speaking to groups of parents, I often recall an experience from my own parenting. When my young family moved into military housing, my children were excited to discover a new kind of "weed" flourishing in our back yard. Those weeds were actually artichokes.

Because artichokes require two years to bloom, I realized that whoever planted these artichokes did not know who would eat them, but they planted them anyway. Perhaps they didn't even realize it, but those planters left a gift for my family and for our entire neighborhood. I believe that we all are called to plant seeds of kindness and understanding, even though we might not ever see the results.

As an author and parent educator, I recognize very few people will read this book. I also recognize that of those who buy this book, only a few will read it. Of those who do read it, an even smaller percentage will accept this calling to teach tomorrow's leaders. But I have a calling to write and share and teach this message anyway. The very act of buying this book and choosing to read it is a response to *your* calling to be a better parent and to teach and share what you learn each day.

I envision YOUR children when I write.

They may not be "my kids" and yet they are. We are all connected and operate in a physical and spiritual realm of community. If I can influence you to be more mindful in your parenting skills, it will affect how all the children you encounter will act. Like ripples in the stream, we all radiate out from each experience and enrich or diminish the lives of others.

You are called to be the kind of teacher and leader to give your children the skills, attitude and eagerness to learn for the love of learning, to become critical thinkers and ask, "Why not?" As your children enter school and become leaders to other youngsters, those seeds you planted in your own garden will spread to benefit your entire community.

You are truly a blessed teacher and mentor. Thank you for the important work you do.

Ready for School

Kindergarten is an exciting and critical time in your child's development and growth. It is hard to relinquish your child to a school and a different teacher. Hopefully, this new influence will continue the pursuit of education that you have already established at home.

Each teacher and classroom will have his or her own style and methods of making learning exciting. One kindergarten teacher may comment on the green grass. Another will pick a blade and share it with the group of hungry-to-learn children. They will describe its various colors, its flexibility, its root system, and its ability to make a noise when held in the lips while blowing out.

This extraordinary teacher can spend hours on a blade of grass and involve every single child in the class. This fun session will become a living lesson and each will personalize it in a different way. Each child in that class will not only discover basic facts about this ground cover, but how it affects him as an individual.

His senses will become engaged, his feelings involved, his thinking expanded, his vocabulary enlarged and his appreciation for the teacher and the lesson will be limitless.

As a parent, you will want to get a sense of where your child's teachers are coming from, and try to establish a partnership for the good of the whole class as well as your child. Most teachers are compassionate, kind and dedicated. If you find that a teacher has an agenda or bias that creates an atmosphere where learning is stressful and the class community is polarized, take necessary steps to advocate for the class to the administration.

Rhymers are Readers

Do you want to guarantee your child will be a good reader? The solution is **Nursery Rhymes**. Surprised? Don't be. The reasons these little stories, poems and songs have been popular for generations is because they reinforce early reading skills and positively influence the developing brain and personality of the child.

Nursery rhymes are fun. Kids love to recite them and they provide a warm, nurturing experience between the caring adult and the child. They open doors of conversation and connection as they are shared. Here is a quote from one of my favorite children's authors and reading expert, Mem Fox.

"Experts in literacy and child development have discovered that if children know eight nursery rhymes by heart by the time they're four years old, they're usually among the best readers by the time they're eight." [Fox, M. (2001). Reading Magic. San Diego, CA: Harcourt.]

(Be sure to check out her book about <u>Winnefrid Gordon McDonald Partridge</u>. It is a classic to teach your children about compassion and how memory works. Four stars and two thumbs up.)

Mother Goose is Great

Here are just a few things you and your child will share as you share favorite nursery rhymes:

- Social routine and taking turns, which is vital to developing conversational skills;
- Repetition, which will help the child learn but also to anticipate what is coming next;
- Even very little kids, or those who have special needs respond to rhythm and tone before they understand language;
- Language skills and vocabulary as you talk, sing and read about the pretend people in the rhyme;
- Voice modulation and facial expressions;
- Early reading skills. Start at the left margin and move your finger along the text as you read to your child. You can teach your child to use his "finger tool," or pointer finger, to follow along the text as well. This prepares them for the written word;
- Story sequence of what happens in the beginning, middle and end of story;
- Creative drama when the kids get to act out the nursery rhymes;
- Early math concepts. Many of the popular nursery rhymes use counting or describe sizes like many, few and plenty, which builds a foundation for math skills;

Emma Lou, 5 years old -
The games and dances we do in school
are fun. My favorite is when we sing and
do the hokey-pokey or duck, duck, goose. I
like to move around a lot.

Read, Talk and Sing

The more you read, talk and sing with your child, the more confident the child will be about the opportunities to increase their learning capacity. I know that is what I talked about with *Raising Smart and Kind Kids: The Baby Years*, and in Raising Smart and Kind Kids: The Toddler Years. Just like our children, we all learn best by repetition. We need to hear the same message over and over, until it becomes part of who we are.

If you commit to a minimum of 20 minutes daily of the following activities, your child will enter Kindergarten with a large vocabulary and love of learning.

Reading! After you read your child a story, hand them the book and encourage them to tell you about it. You will be amazed at what words, facial expressions and tone of voice they remember.

Reading never ceases to be a connection for our family. What an absolute joy to be reading the same book as your teen-age grandkids. Of course, they may have to explain some of the "buzz words." But sharing a book has opened amazing conversations that span generation, cultures and value systems.

Singing and dancing is such a fun way of communication for building community. Our adult children still love it when we call to sing "Happy Birthday" to them. And we love it when our grandchildren call and sing to us or Skype themselves doing a "love dance." Music is the universal language, and a smile is the universal signal for friendship and acceptance. It is understood when no other language connects and unites us as one.

Talking is one of the best ways to connect with your kids. Talking and listening. Then listening some more. Some great conversation starters: "I wonder what would happen if………." Or "ask me any question in the world and see if you can stump me?" "Tell me about what kind of a friend you will be when you go to college?" "What is your favorite part of your hand? Why?"

You are helping them to be critical thinkers and to use their creative abilities and incredible imaginations.

Mandie, 5 years old
I love the job of playing with our dog,
Rosie, and remembering to feed and water
her every day. I hate doing "Scoop the
poop," but Dad says that is part of having a
dog in the family.

Responsibility, Respect and Resilience
— The other 3 R's

We all want our kids and grandkids to grow up with confidence in the future and their ability to make the world a better place. It is the wish of all caring adults that kids develops life skills of *responsibility, respect and resilience* in order to contribute and share their talents and skills with others. These life skills don't just happen when a child turns six, or sixteen or sixty. They happen by gradually adding experience and observation. Like all skills, it takes practice and a commitment to the end goal.

If your child is a typical active preschooler, he may be interested in learning the skill of riding a two-wheeler bike. Don't worry if by age six, they show no interest in this activity. Our second daughter did not want to learn to ride a bike until she was ten, and she still turned out to be a wonderful woman who makes great decisions and lots of money.

For many kids, however, learning to ride without training wheels is a milestone, a big transition and a touch point in learning and growing up. As his parents, you want to be careful not to criticize or condemn, but to encourage forward movement and ultimate mastery of the skill.

Just like the skills of gaining confidence, playing piano, learning to read etc., bike riding is hard at first, but after a few bumps and bruises, it will become second nature to your child. This interest will become hard-wired into their brain, just like all of the other skills they are developing.

Enhance but Don't Enable

I wish I could convince parents that their job is to enhance or add to the formal education their child gets in school. If your daughter read about frogs in school today, parents and extended family can enhance her learning by asking her to teach them about frogs and then inviting her to learn more about frogs together.

Learning really sticks when you have the opportunity to teach it to someone else.

It is important to advocate for your child, without becoming "helicopter parents" who hover over their children and save them from any unpleasantness in life. Every parent in the world, including me, hates to send his or her babies out into the cold, cruel world. We want to wrap them in a security blanket and snuggle them close and protect them from ever getting hurt feelings or hurt fingers. The sad truth is that enabling them to stay helpless does not serve the child or the world they ultimately must maneuver.

Our job as parents is to help our children help themselves. We want them to become self-reliant, responsible adults. In fact, my first book Kids, Chores & More was written not because I was a parent educator and mom, but because we owned businesses. We were appalled at the kids (and adults) who wanted and needed work, but were unable to be self-directed and problem solvers.

As business owners we had neither the time, nor energy, to re-parent an individual who had never been taught to think or act on his own. Trust me.

Help your child to help himself and they will learn the life skills of Respect, Responsibility, and Resilience.

You will be so glad you did.

Learning Styles

In his landmark book, Frames of Mind. The theory of multiple intelligences, developmental psychologist Howard Gardner described seven distinct learning styles. But I have found that by paying attention to just three, you can determine your child's main learning style. Watch him as he learns a new skill. Can you determine which way he learns and processes information?

When is she most successful? Does she learn more quickly from visual cues (needs to see it demonstrated), auditory (hears what you want and responds easily), or tactile (prefers to do it by herself, very hands on)?

A fun activity I use in my parenting classes is to have everyone close their eyes and then I say the words-apple, apple, and apple. I then ask what image came into their mind or what physical experience occurred in their body.

Those who are auditory (10%) usually see the word spelled out or they will repeat the word. They learn best by hearing the words spoken. Those who are kinesthetic (10%) will envision an apple pie, apple tree or Apple computer. They learn best by doing the task, perhaps even finding a new and better way to do it. Many will say they could smell the apple pie, feel the apple peeling or taste the applesauce.

Those who are visual (80%) will usually see an apple, multiple apples or another kind of fruit. But they see a picture in their minds that is clear and easily recognizable. We use the words spoken to construct a visual representation of what the words represent to us.

- **Auditory learners** remember best by talking out loud or repeating instructions back to you. They may have trouble with written manuals. Auditory learners may talk to themselves as they work out problems.

- **Visual learners** easily remember visual details and prefer to see what they are learning. They love it when you paint a "word picture" describing what the end product will look like. They may have difficulty following lectures and may appear to be daydreaming when someone else is talking.

- **Kinesthetic or tactile learners** prefer activities that they can do while they are learning. They are "on-the-job" learners. Tactile learners like to touch things in order to learn about them and can concentrate best when they have something to touch or play with (small ball or rock) while listening to a lecture. They also like to move around when talking or listening.

Often, kinesthetic or tactile learners may be labeled with Attention Deficit Disorder because they learn best while in motion.

Fortunately, psychologists and teachers are finding lots of new techniques to help these active youngsters learn.

A wonderful book to share with young kinetic learners is It's Hard to Be a Verb by Julia Cook.

Another tool used in classrooms is the Disc'o'Sit Jr. inflatable chair cushion. This cushion offers "active sitting," which strengthens the muscles that support the spine.

Use when a greater range of motion and sensory input is needed. It is very helpful for decreasing fidgeting and increasing awareness.

Make Learning Styles Work for You

While most of us use a combination of all three learning styles, your child may have a preferred method of gathering information and processing that information so that it makes sense to him. If he is predominately a kinetic leaner, make sure the pre-school or kindergarten teacher teaches him in that way.

Do what you can to insure his success in early learning.

Does your teaching style match your child's learning style? Understanding how your child processes information will assist you to help them with their homework or to figure out a concept or lesson.

You might be able to present information in a way that they can grasp. You will also help him to adapt to teachers who use different methods of getting a lesson across to a room full of wiggly children.

My husband Dwain is very auditory and when he hears an instruction, he is able to remember and perform the task. Our son Andy, who is now studying architecture, is very kinesthetic and needs to be able to see, feel and touch a project before he could perform the task.

Until we recognized the difference between Dwain and Andy's learning styles, it caused lots of friction between the two. What Dwain was asking was not coming through in a way that Andy could understand. By considering Andy's learning style, Dwain was able to tweak how he presented instructions.

Ahhh, peace and less frustration for father and son.

Andy 28 years old –
My favorite and best teachers are my older
sisters. They taught me how to read, play
music, ride bikes and develop a love of
learning. I still love to share books, ideas
and thoughts with them.

Critical Thinking Skills

Critical thinking is not just about memorization but also about implementation. How to put what you know into real life situations?

Scholastic Magazines for Parents has some ideas on teaching problem solving and developing good thinking skills:

"Critical thinking has become a buzzword in education. In the past, the emphasis in classrooms has been on imparting information and content — the times tables or the capitals of the United States, for example. In recent years, however, there's been a shift toward teaching *critical thinking*, a skill that elevates thinking beyond memorization into the realm of analysis and logic.
Put another way, critical thinking is about knowing how to think, not what to think. Teachers use a number of techniques to help students learn critical thinking, starting as early as kindergarten and ramping up especially in 2nd grade and beyond. Below are a few of the methods educators employ; you can try them at home to help your child become a critical thinker.

- **Critical thinking: Ask open-ended questions.** Asking questions that don't have one right answer encourages children to respond creatively without being afraid of giving the wrong answer.
- **Critical thinking: Categorize and classify.** Classification plays an important role in critical thinking because it requires identification and sorting according to a rule, or set of rules, that kids must discover, understand, and apply. If you play classification games at home, be sure to follow up the activity with questions about the similarities and differences between

the groups. You can sort everything from dirty laundry to Legos to produce to doll clothes to promote critical thinking.

- **Critical thinking: Work in groups.** In a group setting, students are exposed to the thought processes of their peers. Thus, they can begin to understand how others think and that there are multiple ways of approaching problems — not just one correct way.
- **Critical thinking: Make decisions.** Help your child consider pros and cons, but don't be afraid to let her make a wrong choice. Then evaluate the decision later. Ask your child, "How do you feel about your decision? What would you do differently next time?"
- **Critical thinking: Find patterns.** Whatever you're doing, whether it's going to the park or watching television, encourage your child to look for patterns or make connections for critical thinking practice. For example, relate a favorite television show to a real-life situation. Or, while driving in the car, have your child identify different shapes in roads signs and in the windows and roofs of passing houses.

It might be tempting to pass off the critical thinking buzz as just another fad in education. However, most teachers disagree. It's still important for your child to know his multiplication tables, but it's just as vital for him to know how and when to use them."

My own take on this is that problem solvers will always be needed in the world of work. Employers would much rather hire people with a 'can-do attitude" than one with the aptitude of one certain subject.

If we always encourage a love of learning in children and ourselves we influence, the world will be a welcoming place to exist and flourish.

How to Think, Not What to Think

Critical thinking is about knowing how to think, not what to think. We want our children to become problem solvers and to find new and innovative ways to find solutions. We want to make sure their pre-school and elementary years are spent in an environment that allows for expansive learning experiences and not just teaching to the test.

Teachers and parents can use a number of different ways to help children help themselves and become more self-reliant.

Hopefully we have encouraged our babies and toddlers (see Raising Smart and Kind Kids: The Baby Years and Raising Smart and Kind Kids: The Toddler Years) to love to learn.

Why, Why Not and What's Next?

Helping your child develop problem-solving skills is one of your most important tasks. It can also be one of the most frustrating. Many bright children continually ask "why" and "how" and "why not" and "what if." Those who are allowed and encouraged to become problem solvers continually challenge their parents on what they hear, see and are asked to do.

Sally, mom of Gavin, five years old, said: "One day I had reached my last nerve of patience and when he asked "why?" for the 400th time, I just lost it. I told him that he was forbidden to ask why any more that day (I know, but sometimes mothers go a little crazy) and as he was walking away with his head down and lower lip out he turned to me. "Why can't I ask you why anymore?" It ended with a hug and an aspirin.

These incredible spirits are primed to learn and lead. Our job is to keep them safe and open new horizons so they can gain experience and empathy. What they are going to be has not been invented yet, and they most likely will invent it and teach others.

The children being born in this generation are frequently called "Indigo Children." They have been exposed to technology in the womb and so are already familiar with gadgets, electronics and global communication.

For more information on this subject, you may want to read my article called Indigo Children, Born To Lead - Hard to Manage

Teachers, neighbors, parents and all other caring adults form a partnership to raise smart & kind kids. Everyone in the village or community wants successful kids who feel accepted and acknowledged.

What Teachers Want From Parents

In visiting with many teachers, not only those who taught our children, but others in our circle of friends, family and community; I have learned some basic ideas. I hope you will find them useful and want to add to the list.

- **Be involved with your child's education.** Enhance learning at home. You don't have to be the room parent, unless you want to. But be available to help not just your child, but also the classroom.

- **Read, sing and talk to your child.** Read bedtime stories and tell family stories. Talk about how things are made. Why we do the things we do. How things work. Why people in books and life made the choices they made. Talk and listen to your children and all children.

- **Set a good example.** Let your children see you reading, discussing and researching topics that interest you. Don't let your television or video games raise your child.

- **Encourage the love of learning.** Parents who believe that education is an on-going activity will have bright, critical thinking children who recognize that there are many layers of learning.

- **Encourage academics.** Help them to understand that you want them to do the best they can. If they learn better in a different way, then communicate that to the teacher.

- **Set realistic goals.** If a child is involved with too many activities and yet is being pressured to perform academically, it may be too much. Be selective in activities and don't expect perfection in any area.

- **Call teachers early if there is a problem.** Don't wait until parent-teacher conference. If there is a situation where your child does not understand math or reading, get help before it becomes overwhelming for the child.

- **Assume personal responsibility for teaching your child.** Children who know basic rules of dignity and respect for others are well liked and accepted. Those life-skills should be taught and practiced on a daily basis. A good teacher can enhance what the child has learned at home, but does not have time to re-parent.

Starting as early as kindergarten and ramping up especially in 2nd grade and beyond, those gifted teachers will encourage your child to build on the learning skills you have already talked about. If they are not getting the basics, it makes it very difficult to go to the next step in the curriculum.

Erin, 4 year old –
I love recess at preschool. It is fun to run
and chase my friends. It gets all my
wiggles out so I can really listen to the
teacher.

Competence and Confidence

Children who experience being loved and accepted as they are, not as they may become if they just try harder, have a priceless advantage in confidence and courage. Those who have a sure knowledge they are loved unconditionally are not afraid to fail occasionally.

. They have learned it is okay to make mistakes or do things the wrong way while they are learning.

Bright children generally have more friends, enjoy school and lead a happier life than those of average intelligence and a dislike for learning. But that is not true for all children. As I researched for my book The Left Out Child-The Importance of Friendship, I was struck by how many children could read and understand Shakespeare or Harry Potter, but could not read and understand facial expressions or body language of friends. They did not grasp the concept of social skills, physical and emotional boundaries, and how not to appear "a know-it-all" or teacher's pet.

There are many ways to teach social skills and the ability to make and keep friends. This is the perfect time to teach empathy and to help them understand the feelings and emotions of others.

Bullies or Buddies?

1. **Kelso's Choice** is a wonderful <u>anti-bullying program</u> designed for elementary schools. It assists young children to recognize and realize that if you have a BIG problem, you tell an adult you trust. If you have a small problem, then you try at least two of Kelso's choices:

- Find something else to do. Go to another game.

- Share and take turns.

- Talk it out. Use "I" statements like, "I feel angry when you take all the good cars to play with," or "I need you to share some with me."

- Take a time out to think. Just walk away.

- Ignore what is going on. Just go to a place in your imagination and think of other things.

- Tell them to stop. You can do this with words or with holding your hand up in a stop position.

- Apologize for your part in the conflict.

- Make a deal. Do rock, paper, scissors, or come up with a win-win solution or at least a fair solution.

- Say, "I have to wait to cool off."

Kids with special needs may require extra help and for you to model the behavior a few times until they understand.  This program is available at <u>www.kelsoschoices.net</u> and I highly recommend it.

Logan, 10 years old –

"I liked learning about Kelso's Choices. It helps me to stop and think if something is a small problem or a big problem. When I decide it really is just a small problem and I make a choice to ignore someone who is being rude, I really do feel good."

2. **Make sure your children understand your love is unconditional** and is not predicated on what they accomplish or do. Children need to be taught the skills of reading non-verbal communication clues or interpreting verbal messages correctly. They may misconstrue your cranky mood as anger toward them. Reassure them that adults have lots on their minds and children are not responsible for bad things that happen.

3. **Special Play Time** Learning to play with your child is not always easy, nor is allowing time to just "be." Do not question or give directions if you are invited to play. Allow them to take the lead. Be enthusiastic about his interests. You will want to check out the affordable and effective guide of 77 Ways to Have Fun with Your Family for Free

Teach Non-Verbal Clues

Pre-school and early schools are a wide-open window of opportunity to teach empathy and compassion. In doing research for my books on bullying, I learned that if children do not embrace empathy and recognize the feelings of other people now, it would require adult intervention later on.

4. **Recognizing and naming emotions is an important skill** that is needed throughout life. Learning to correctly interpret feelings is easier when you are young and have someone to give you guidance. Look at pictures in magazines or people watch in the mall. Ask your child, "What do you think they are feeling?" "What do you think they are thinking about?" "How do you look when you are sad?" "How do you look when you are worried?" "How about when you are surprised?" Confused, afraid, embarrassed, nervous, full of giggles, proud, see an animal that is hurt?

Emily, 6 years old –
"Sometimes my mom
says she isn't mad but
her face looks mad."

5. **Play What if?** "What if" is a wonderful game to help gauge the understanding and coping skills of your child. It is also a valuable tool to teach problem solving and looking at options. As you are driving to school or taking a walk, take turns asking each other about imaginary

situations and what you would do. For example: "What if we got separated at the grocery store and you couldn't find me. What are three different things you could do?" Don't downplay the poor choices (walking home, climbing a tower and looking for you). Rather encourage the wise ones and help them to understand there are always options

Ridge, 7 years old –

"My mom said that I was really smart to think that if I was lost in the Mall to go to the clock tower, because it was right in the middle of the Mall. Or if I was lost in the grocery store to go to the check out and tell the lady. She said she would come right there to start looking. But I won't get lost again. Now I am older and smarter."

Teach Diversity

Children who have a love of learning will also have a natural enthusiasm for sharing. Part of your job as an adult is to teach humility and a non-judgment attitude toward others who do not appreciate your interests.

Emma 4 –
"I love going to International Day at the University. We all get something to eat from a different country and then share it. The program is fun. I can't wait to be a foreign exchange student."

6. **Invite and Introduce.** Share meals and play dates with other families so your child will be comfortable around different ages and types of people.

7. **Words Can Hurt.** Help your child to be aware of how much more alike we are than different. Help them understand why offensive words or jokes can hurt someone's feelings.

Teach Responsibility

Not assuming personal responsibility is a major irritant of mine; as a mom, teacher, landlord and business owner. And I don't think I am alone in this. When gathering with parents it is their top concern. As well as teachers, who shake their head at all the excuses and blaming that goes on with students...and parents. When I meet with other business owners they say it is their top headache when employees do not take responsibility for their jobs and choices.

This was the primary motivation that prompted my book <u>Kids,</u> <u>Chores & More</u>.   Kids who are responsible for chores, personal care and age appropriate tasks do better in school and life.

Let the children participate in the planning of which jobs get done, when they get done and what happens if they are not done. Once a schedule has been agreed on, stick to it. The most important word in parenting is consistency. It is easier for your child to be responsible if the task is defined and expected.

Every child and adult in the family has responsibility for making the house run smoother. For more information on this, visit http://www.ResponsibleChildren.com to find age appropriate chores to build cooperation.

8. **Dinner and sharing time.** Just as parents have "jobs" they go to each day, so do children. Their job is to learn about all the interesting things going on in the world and to share that wonder and excitement with the family. May I suggest you establish a family dinner hour with no electronics or interruptions? This time of sharing is vital to the unity and camaraderie the family feels as they download all the stress from the day and take time upload the support from each other.

9. **Homework at home.** Homework is a child's work and establishing a time after a comfortable dinner and clean up is a great habit to begin even before homework is assigned. If your child recognizes that after dinner, he will be reading or working on writing or doing art, he will come to associate that time as a scheduled activity.

10. **Lost jackets and misplaced gloves.** I know you are going to scream when I say this, but; count on losing a jacket or two each year and just budget for it. If you get furious when the weather changes and your child leaves his jacket or sweater on the playground, you can count on being furious at least a few times a week. How about deciding to save your screaming for something really important and just know that someone else who probably needed the jacket is now warm. Your child does not forget things on purpose, but sometimes we all "just forget."

11. **Systemize and make life simpler.** Set up systems to help your child be organized and more responsible for his possessions. Library books in one place. Sports gear in one place. I am going to write an eBook on 77 Ways To Organize Your Kids soon, so watch for it.

12. **Date, time and place.** Keep a family calendar posted, so that everyone knows who goes where, when and how they are going to get there. The more systems you have in place, the less stress your family will feel.

Teach Respect

Respect is a two-way street and very important life-skill. If we want to receive respect from others, then we must learn to give it to those we encounter on a daily basis. When we respect someone, we treat them with kindness; thoughtfulness and try to make them feel appreciated and heard. The message we want our children to learn is that to respect someone is to give an unspoken acknowledgement of, "I see you and I value you."

13. **Establish rules about privacy and interrupting conversations.** Help them develop techniques to let

adults know they have something important to share without being obnoxious.

14. **Teach social skills and table manners.** Help them to hold the utensils correctly and to wait for others to start eating. Assist them in being able to measure what an appropriate bite of food is (which my grandsons assume is half a hamburger at once.) and how to chew with their mouth closed.

15. **Model respect for people, places and things.** Explain about how we have a stewardship to care for the things we have been given. Show how to take good care of our toys and clothing and showing respect for the many blessings that we have. Showing respect for the earth is by not littering or taking our community for granted.

16. **Quiet time and noisy time.** Teach your child to recognize the time to run and shout and the time to walk softly, speak quietly and to respect the feelings of others around you. I always keep a package of pipe cleaners from the dollar store in my purse.

David, 4 years old
"My worst chore is unloading the
dishwasher because you have to be careful
that the door doesn't scratch your leg when
you go around it."

These are the best quiet toys ever invented. Little fingers can form people, towns, rockets or jewelry. Their imagination is in full force and their mouths and feet are quiet.

Teach Resiliency

17. **Stronger than you think.** Nature can teach so much about cycles of life and that events really are temporary. It is important to focus on the present, because tomorrow will change just as plants will come up in the spring. When your family is going through tough times, go out in nature and talk about strength- the strength to start again. Talk about flexibility and watch a willow tree bend and sway, but bounce back when the wind stops blowing. Be sure to see Out of Balance? Be a Bounce-Back Person, my best-selling book that will help the whole family become more resilient in times of adversity.

18. **Help your child build a safety net** of people who care about his success in life. As a counting game when he is stressed and a meltdown is just about to happen (usually in the produce aisle of the market or in church when he wants to write in the hymnal), whisper the names of all the people who love him. There is a community of people who think he is a pretty special kid. He needs to know that if he is ever in a bad situation that he can count on those caring adults to help.

19. **My Private Parts.** It is important to talk about how people may truly love you and yet may ask you to do something that is not in your best interest. Sexual abuse and molestations are rarely from strangers in the park, but someone who is known and trusted by the family.

My Private Parts is a wonderful picture book by Diane Hanson and her 4-year-old daughter.

It is available at www.ArtichokePress.com

My book about <u>Caution Without Fear-Aware but Not Afraid</u> helps parents teach their kids that adults are supposed to protect kids, not use devious ways to get them to do things that are uncomfortable or harmful.

The wider the village of caring adults a child has, the more they can find other helpful grownups to talk to. Sometimes you may have to name the people who would help if he were ever in a difficult situation or had a hard decision to make.

As much as we wish our children would turn to us for advice, usually they are afraid they might get in trouble, or it would add to our burdens or sadly, that we would not believe them.

20. **Situations are Temporary.** Talk about how our feelings can change just like the seasons change. It is fine to stand in sadness or disappointment and feel the feelings, but know we have the ability to choose when we are ready to change to a better feeling and attitude.

Lacey, 7 years old -

"When my brother Lucas got leukemia
when he was 12, our whole family had to
move to Seattle to be near his hospital.
We lived in the Ronald McDonald house. It
was a really scary time. My parents kept
saying, "We will be alright.
This is a tough time, but we can do it."
He is getting better now."

21. **Disappointment and Discouragement.** If your child is expressing disappointment in a lack of playmates, you will want to check out http://www.TheLeftOutChild.com. Friendship is a skill, just like any other skill and can be taught and mastered with practice and encouragement.

Do not confuse a shy child with a self-contained child. Many children who have had lots of intellectual stimulus are simply bored with the pre-school games and prefer to play alone. The social scene will even out midyear.

Transition Time

Transition time can be one of the toughest adjustments of life. Whether that transition is leaving Mom to go to school, leaving favorite toys at Dad's house when it is Mom's weekend, leaving nap time to go nap-less, moving to a new house, a new teacher, or even to a new bed, it involves a learning situation and change. It is hard to know what to expect.

As parents, you can both make the transition an adventure and help your child take a part in planning to ease the stress or you can deal with the aftermath.

22. **Reinforce Coping Behaviors.** The key to helping children to become less fearful is to allow them to have some control over the situation. Serve as a home base, but let her venture out and then return to your safety. Make sure you give positive feedback about how well she handled the situation and that you have confidence in her ability to make this transition. If she needs a talisman to reminder of your love and support, perhaps you could paint a small rock to carry in her pocket or remind her that every time she sees the letter C (for courage), you will be thinking of her.

23. **Try to be as consistent in the routine as possible.** Do not make a huge deal out of it and talk it to death. You may make your child afraid or fearful when there is no need. Speak in a matter of fact voice that different situations have different rules and that you will not be able to stay with her. Express confidence in her ability to have fun and find lots of things to do that she can share with you when you reunite later

24. **Keep In Close Touch.** Babies and toddlers require a lot of physical touching and interaction. As pre-school children grow and expand their world, parents tend to touch them less and spend most of the interaction time with giving orders or correcting behavior. Make a conscious effort to give hugs, reassuring pats and kisses to this age child.

Devon, 5 years old
"My dad and I found this little rock that
looks like a heart. He said to keep it in my
pocket and whenever I got lonely for him, I
could rub my fingers on it and remember
how much I love his backrubs."

More Fun Learning Ideas for Preschoolers

Generally, children handle life in a direct reflection of how the parents handle life. Model confidence, courage and an interest in learning about new things, places and opportunities, your child will learn these traits.

25. **Ask Open-Ended Questions.** Asking questions that don't have one right answer encourages children to respond creatively without being afraid of giving the wrong answer. Ask a lot of, "what do you think?" Help them realize there are always at least five solutions to every situation. Ask, "What else might work?"

26. **Not Just One Solution.** In a group setting, students are exposed to brainstorming. Thus, they can begin to understand how others think and that there are multiple ways of approaching problems — not just one correct way. The best way may be a combination of ideas. Help them be respectful of other's opinions and ideas.

27. **Find a Face.** From early childhood, youngsters love to look at human faces. Encourage them to find "faces" in inanimate objects as well – for example, car headlights are eyes and the grill is a grinning mouth. This is a fun way to develop critical thinking while passing time – in waiting rooms, restaurants, as you navigate the grocery store, etc.

28. **Make Decisions.** Help your child consider pros and cons, but don't be afraid to let her make a wrong choice. Then evaluate the decision later. Ask your child, "How do you feel about your decision? What would you do differently next time?" **Reassure her or him that it is**

okay to make a mistake, which is how we learn. Mistakes are actually valuable so we know different ways to do it next time.

29. **Categorize and Classify.** You can sort everything from dirty laundry to Legos to produce to doll clothes to promote critical thinking. Help them problem solve which pile of dirty clothes does a blue and white striped shirt go in. Why? Noticing what is similar and what is different. What goes together and what does not belong are all simple games to help them recognize patterns. Always follow up with questions about what helped them to solve the problem. Encourage their method of working out the problem and finding solutions.

30. **Find Patterns for** critical thinking practice; help your child be aware. Help them look for triangles in nature. Relate a favorite television show to a real-life situation. Or, while driving in the car, have your child identify different shapes in roads signs.

31. **Dress Up and Let's Pretend.** This is a prime age for imagination and role-playing. Listen to the conversations and try not to be involved unless asked. If you hear lots of

bossiness and negative comments, you may want to examine if they heard it originally from you.

32. **Plant a Garden Inside or Out.** Marigolds are pretty resilient and so are radishes and parsley. You may be stumped on what to expect as a family contribution from your child. You will find excellent ideas and suggestions for helping children to gain competence and life skills at http://www.ResponsibleChildren.com

33. **Reuse.** Help your child understand that every time you reuse something for a craft project, you are doing something good for the earth.

34. **Recycle.** Children in this age group are environmental conscious and can probably teach you some things about how to recycle. Have him instruct the family at a family council. Perhaps he could be the team leader for recycle activities.

35. **Regift.** Service to others is the bedrock of civilization. Too many toys or clothes do not make a happy child; they make a confused and overwhelmed child. Help your child simplify so that others can share your blessings

36. **Music Appreciation.** If you want your child to enjoy a particular kind of music, play it in the background as you cook together or eat dinner. Those are usually pleasant memories and he will associate the music with a happy time.

37. **Teach Manners with Ditties and Silly songs.** When soup is served sing: "Like a little ship going out to sea, I dip my spoon away from me."

38. **Set the Table.** Left has four letters and so does fork. The fork goes to the left of the plate as you are looking down at it. Knife has five letters and so does right, so the knife goes to the right of the plate, as does the spoon.

39. **Puppet Shows.** This is a great vehicle for speech development, creative thoughts and developing imagination. Allow your child to make puppets from all the unmatched pairs of socks (or buy puppets at a yard sale.) She may want to invite a friend (lots of play dates at this age) and print up tickets and a program.

40. **Read the Signs.** Help your child to read frequently seen signs, such as STOP, EXIT, ONE WAY.

41. **Write Your Child's Life Story.** One of my most valuable treasures is a book I co-authored with a granddaughter called, "*My Life So Far-By Melissa, age 6*." She stood by my computer and answered questions and told me fun memories. My book on writing memoirs for adults, Leave a Living Legacy, offers valuable ideas for those who would like to write their own life stories.

42. **Money Magic.** Kids love to play with coins. Buy a roll of nickels and a couple of rolls of pennies or let them count the money in your change box (you know, the one where you dump the change from your pocket each night). As

your child begins to sort, count or stack the coins to develop fine motor skills, you will be surprised how much fun they will have. Or, they can use their magnifying glass to find the year and the mint where the coin was made. Can you find a coin that was made the year your child was born? When you were born? When your father was born? Talk about how money is made and the many uses of money. How many quarters to buy a toy?

43. **Set Up a Store.** Save empty cartons, containers and plastic bottles. They can use cardboard boxes for store shelves and a wagon for a shopping cart. Encourage them to make signs and specials. Perhaps they can make money out of construction paper and use the math skills developed above.

44. **Build a "Feeling Tree or Chart."** As you identify feeling words and emotions draw, a face representing how that feels to the child. Write the word out and find pictures to glue next to the word. When the child needs a prompt to explain how he is feeling, praise him for choosing the right word and recognizing that he can choose other reactions.

45. **Pieces of Paper.** Everyone loves to tear paper, but to encourage it, what fun! This strengthens small muscles and also builds creativity in learning about tactile surfaces. Suggest that the child tear up lots of papers of different consistency and texture in small, medium and large pieces. Now make a collage with a poster board, glue and a box of paper pieces. You could also throw them in the air and pretend it is snowing. Of course you will be vacuuming up the scraps for years.

46. **Preparing Meals.** A simple way to teach nutrition is to say there must be at least four different colors on each plate for a meal.

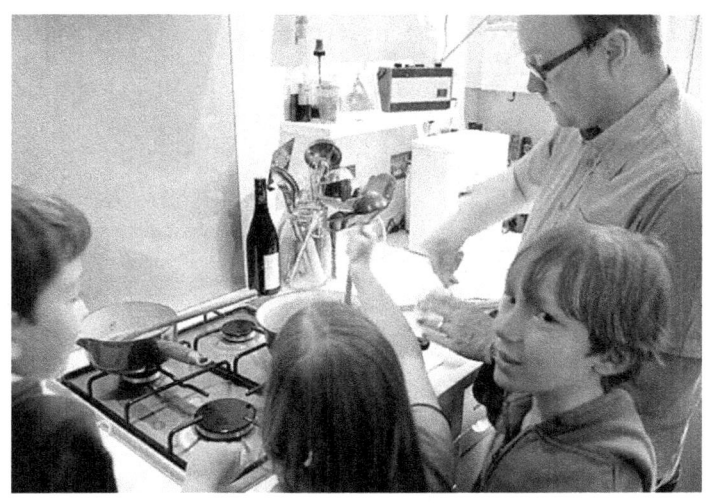

47. **Rather than becoming frustrated** when your child doesn't seem to "get it" remember that learning takes place over a long period of time and it is a process not an end product.

48. **Memory Game.** Put ten small items on a tray, cover with a dishcloth. Let the child look for one minute and then cover it up again and then remove from the room. How many can he remember? Does it get better when he has longer to look, or sees the items in a pattern? Now, it is only fair that he be able to play the game with you.

49. **Make a Message Box or Communication Log.** Sometimes it is easier to say things in writing. Whether it is to leave little reminders or messages to express your love, this is an excellent way to supplement your communication with your child.

50. **I Have a Dream.** Every night before bedtime, encourage your child to tell you what they plan to dream about that night. Allow them to use their imagination and only interfere if you feel the dream might be scary. If so, explore what is going on in the day-to-day life of your

child. If not, ask the next morning what she actually dreamed about.

Thank you for spending this small period of time with me.

Please know how much I appreciate the important work that you are doing with your children and the other children in your circle of love.

Blessings and best wishes,

Judy H. Wright aka Auntie

Artichoke

PS: Did you find value in this book? Please leave a review on Amazon, Goodreads or YELP. Reviews help others to find solutions to their problems. Thanks so much.

About The Author

Who is Judy H. Wright *aka Auntie Artichoke?*

& What's with the Artichoke?

 Judy is a parent educator, family coach, and personal historian who has written more than 20 books, hundreds of articles and speaks internationally on family issues, including care giving. Trained as a ready to learn consultant, she works with Head Start organizations and child care resource centers. She also volunteers time writing end-of-life stories for Hospice.

She and Dwain, her husband of 40 years, have six grown children and seven grandchildren. They consider their greatest success in life that their children like themselves and each other. The honorary title of "Auntie" is given in many cultures to the wise women who guide and mentor others in life.

The artichoke also became a teaching lesson when Judy, with her young family, moved into military housing in California to find Artichokes in their yard. Given that it takes two years for the vegetable to flower, the original gardener never got to see the seeds of her labor. Many times, people feel our actions and reactions in life we will never meet, but we plant the seeds of kindness anyway.

The symbol of the artichoke has great meaning in her teaching and writing. As she works with families, she sees frequently only the outer edges are exposed and can be prickly, hard to open and sometimes bitter to the taste. They are closed to new ideas or methods. Many families prefer the known to the unknown, even when the old patterns and skills are not serving them well.

But as you expose the artichoke and people to warmth, caring, and time, gradually the leaves begin to open and expose the real treasure—the heart.

You will enjoy Judy's approachable manner, wonderful storytelling and common-sense solutions gleaned from working with hundreds of families and organizations just like yours. Your encounter with Judy will leave you feeling inspired, entertained and especially motivated. Visit Judy's website for excellent references and a full listing of books, workshop topics, tele-classes and testimonials.

To make arrangements for your group or organization to enjoy having Judy present a keynote address, workshop or training session, please contact her at:

Judy H. Wright aka Auntie Artichoke,

The Storytelling Trainer

(406) 549-9813,

Email: Judy@ArtichokePress.COM

www.ArtichokePress.Com

"Finding the heart of the story in the journey of life."

Free eBook at www.UseEncouragingWords.Com

"Visiting with Judy is like having a cup of tea with a loving auntie."
"We are all grateful for the incredible work you do to birth these stories."

Encouraging Words and Phrases To Empower You and Your Child

© Judy Helm Wright aka "Auntie Artichoke"
http://www.AskAuntieArtichoke.com

1. You are one smart cookie.
2. You break a hard job in smaller tasks- good thinking.
3. Just being around you can brighten my day.
4. Can I give you a hug for your effort?
5. That was a great answer-shows you know how to think problems through.
6. You have a good heart. I really appreciate that.
7. That was thoughtful of you to share with your brother.
8. You are right. Thanks for explaining that to me. Now I see your point of view.
9. You have a wonderful imagination.
10. You have got it now. Proud of you for keeping on till you figured it out.
11. That was a great try. Nobody masters things on the first try. We all have to practice.
12. Wow, that is neat. I am impressed.

13. Honestly, I just think about you and I get a smile on my face.

14. I really like you. You really are a good person to have by your side.

15. That was very nice of you. You have a good heart. Thanks.

16. Exceptional!

17. What careful work. I can see that this project matters to you.

18. That is a great idea. Tell me how you thought of it.

19. Sometimes I am busy at work and I think of you and I just start smiling.

20. Wow. You are very artistic. Tell me what the colors mean to you.

21. Thank you for being honest.

22. I support you in your endeavors.

23. Just know that I am always in your corner cheering for you.

24. Keep trying; you are getting much better at this.

25. I've got faith in you. You have succeeded so many other times.

26. You are the greatest.

27. I really admire the way you are concerned about other people's feelings.

28. You are the kind of friend that everyone would like to have.

29. You are on the right track, just keep going.

30. I have been noticing how clever you are at solving problems, bet you can figure this out too.

31. You are very unique and original. There is no else in the world just like you.

32. You have got what it takes to succeed in your heart and your head.

33. What would I ever do without you?

34. That idea sounds great; let's move forward with it.

35. I am proud of your good sportsmanship. Winning is not nearly as important as enjoying yourself   playing the game.

36. Wow, once again I am amazed at the maturity and judgment you show.

37. You were very brave and I admire your courage.

38. You have such a great imagination. You think of things in a very innovative way.

39. You are a beautiful person inside and out.

40. You are kind. You are good and you are important.

41. Keep up the good work. You are really making progress.

42. I like to listen to your ideas; conversations with you always make me think.

43. Dynamite Thinking. When you come up with lots of ideas, it is fun to see you sort through options and find solutions.

44. Hurray for you!

45. I have noticed how polite you are to older people. Thanks for being so considerate.

46. You are a super listener. I noticed how much it meant for your friend to feel like you were really paying attention to what he was sharing.

47. Thanks for doing your chores without being reminded. That shows how responsible you are becoming.

48. You're helpful to the neighbors. I love to hear good reports about your behavior.

49. Thanks for caring and sharing.

50. You are fun to hang around with.

51. It's easy to see how much you have improved. That must feel good to you.

52. In case you have ever wondered, I trust you to tell me the truth and I will promise to tell you the truth.

53. Hey Buddy! Looking good.

54. Hey Good Looking!

55. Thanks for being you.

56. That is a great idea, I am glad you thought of that.

57. I bet you can figure out a system that will make this easier to do.

58. Your acting (singing, whistling, dancing, skipping, hopping etc.) is so enjoyable to watch.

59. That was a great game you played.

60. I really appreciate you staying late to finish up the project.

61. I have been trying to remember all the good things you do instead of criticizing what doesn't get done. I am thrilled at all you accomplish each day. Thanks.

62. I know that was hard for you to do, but I admire your courage.

63. You really have a good head on your shoulders.

64. Have I told you lately how proud of you I am?

65. Have I told you lately how much I love you?

66. You are very respectful. That means a lot to me.

67. You have a special talent at seeing the humor in a situation.

68. You have a special talent in helping others to see alternatives.

69. You do a good job of calming a situation down that might have been exploded.

70. You are very strong, both on the inside of your heart and in your body.

71. I am really proud of you. I always knew you could do it.

72. You are a "good finder" instead of a "nit picker" and I appreciate that.

73. People really appreciate your leadership abilities.

74. You have a unique learning style and can grasp ideas most people miss.

75. No matter where you go or what you do in life, always remember you are loved unconditionally.

76.   I will always be grateful to have you in my life.

77. You are such a neat person. You are just like sunshine to my soul. Thanks for being you.

Encouraging Words and Phrases To Empower You and Your Child

© Judy Helm Wright aka "Auntie Artichoke"
http://www.AskAuntieArtichoke.com

Resources for Parents, Teachers and other Caring Adults

http://www.ArticlesbyJudy.Com   Free   articles   on relationships/parenting/grief/personal development Free to use in your blog-just keep content and contact info intact.

http://www.JudyHWright.Com Personal website for Judy H. Wright, including blog and articles. Connect with Judy for empowerment coaching and inspirational speaking engagements.

http://www.ArtichokePress.Com Main website for Judy H Wright, full listing of books, workshops, radio shows, tele-classes. Free report available.

http://www.BounceBackPerson.Com Site for Judy's latest book, *Out Of Balance? Be a Bounce Back Person*. Includes bonus items.

http://www.EmpowermentWithJudy.Com Mentoring and Mastermind. Not empowerment for Judy or by Judy, but with Judy. Walking life's journey together.

http://www.KidsChoresandMore.Com Site for Judy's book, *Kids, Chores, And More*. Includes bonus items. Free report available.

http://www.TheLeftOutChild.Com Site for the importance of friendship, Sign up for our free e-course

http://www.AskAuntieArtichoke.Com Blog for parenting and relationships. Please leave comments and questions. You will be glad you did.

http://www.IfDeathIsNear.Com Blog for those facing the loss of a loved one.

http://www.DeathOfMyPet.Com Book and bonus items for someone who has lost a beloved pet. Excellent stories and resources for pet lovers.

http://www.CyberbullyingHelp.Com Main site for bullying and cyberbullying assistance. Free report and connections to other blogs and websites. Leave comments and share your story.

http://www.UseEncouragingWords.Com Main site for free e-book on the power of words and communication.

http://www.DisciplineYesPunishNo.Com Site for alternatives to punishment. Transform and strengthen your family connections and communications.

http://www.WelcomeAbundance.Com Methods of earning passive streams of income.

http://www.EncourageSelfConfidence.Com Site for Judy's book, *Using Encouraging Words to Motivate Positive Action* and bonus items about building self-confidence with encouraging words.

http://www.4LifeHappyKids.com/Judy Goal setting and teaching your children the Law of Attraction.

http://www.JudyHWright.com/GiggleBaby Giggle Baby – Find great clothes and creative products for your children

Thank you for joining our community of kind, thoughtful people who want to model and teach kindness, tolerance and respect for all.

www.ingramcontent.com/pod-product-compliance
Lightning Source LLC
Chambersburg PA
CBHW060505290526
45791CB00001B/281